पुरातत्त्व

पुरातत्त्व

PURĀTATTVA

Bulletin of the Indian Archaeological Society

No. 2 1968-69

Editors
A.K. Narain
M. Seshadri
S.B. Deo

Assistant Editors
P.C. Pant
P. Singh

D.K. Printworld (P) Ltd.
New Delhi

Cataloging in Publication Data — DK
[Courtesy : D.K. Agencies (P) Ltd. <docinfo@dkagencies.com>]

Purātattva : bulletin of the Indian Archaeological Society, no. 2, 1968-69 / editors, A.K. Narain, M. Seshadri, S.B. Rao ; assistant editors, P.C. Pant, P. Singh.
p. cm.
Includes bibliographical references.
ISBN 8124602786

1. Archaeology — India — Periodicals. 2. India — Antiquities — Periodicals. 3. India — Civilization — Periodicals. I. Narain, A.K. II. Seshadri, M. III. Rao, S.B. IV. Indian Archaeological Society.

First Reprinted in 2005
ISBN 81-246-0278-6
Price for volume 2 (1968-69): Rs. 600 US $ 30

Reprint authorised by
Indian Archaeological Society
New Delhi - 110 016

The Editors are not responsible for the opinions expressed by the Contributors.

Purātattva is published annually.
Manuscripts (whether in the form of articles or notes or book reviews) offered for publication should be sent to the Editor, Purātattva, Indian Archaeological Society, B-17, Qutab Institutional Area, New Delhi - 110 016.

Published and printed by:
D.K. Printworld (P) Ltd.
'Srikunj,' F-52, Bali Nagar
New Delhi – 110015
Phone : (011) 2545 3975, 2546 6019 Fax : (011) 2546 5926
E-mail : dkprintworld@vsnl.net
www. dkprintworld.com

CONTENTS

Articles

Outlines of the Archaeology of Nepal

by N. R. BANERJEE

Introduction

Archaeology as a discipline of research serves Clio the Muse of History as a handmaiden, for filling gaps that historical records have failed to bridge. Its purpose otherwise is to probe those aspects of human life that are beyond the reach of historical research. It undertakes the task by the study of the standing monuments of art and architecture, and all other relics of human handiwork that can be recovered only by archaeological excavation, and are eventually preserved and displayed in the museums. It also enjoys at once the privilege and responsibility of preserving the rich heritage of the past for posterity, and of course of interpreting it for everyman's comprehension.

Its scope is the entire range of human life and activities extending from the dimmest and remotest past of prehistory, through the intermediate phase of protohistory, both before the age of written records, and the entire gamut of the historical periods reaching almost upto the recent times.

Regardless of the as yet inestimable but surely remote antiquity of Nepal, which has the unique distinction of harbouring the tallest mountains in the world, the archaeology of Nepal is very young, perhaps the youngest in the world. The work in the field is being carried out in the main by the Department of Archaeology, under the Ministry of Education, H.M.G., instituted in 1952. It is of course a rapidly growing organisation and its activities presently cover(i) exploration and excavation of ancient sites, including prehistoric studies, (ii) conservation of ancient monuments, including chemical conservation, (iii) collection and publication of inscriptions and coins, (iv) survey of sculptures and architecture, (v) maintenance of museums, (vi) research and (vii) publication of academic works and technical reports, all in the field of archaeology. The legal aspects of the archaeological work in the country are controlled and governed by the *Prachin Smarak Samrakshan Ain* (Ancient Monuments Preservation Act) of 2013 V.S. (A.D. 1956).

Though it has not yet been possible to isolate all the diverse cultural patterns that may have evolved at one time or other in the vastly variegated terrains of the country through the corridors of time, not to speak of studying them fully, or working out a complete sequence of cultures among them, the work is already on the anvil. The influence of the isolating and mountainous geography of the country with its concomitant ensemble of flora, fauna and climate on the peoples of Nepal throughout her hoary history has been profound. This itself is a clue to the understanding of the patterns of culture that have emerged on the embroidered chessboard of many hues that Nepal represents, imbibing, combining and welding local and exotic elements together.

Scarcely more than a beginning has been made in the study of the lives of the diverse peoples that constitute the Nepalese populace, but there can be no doubt that they bear echoes till this day of the lives of the long last past and should provide useful guidelines in the study of the ancient beginnings and later moorings.

The Kaleidoscope of the Sequence of Cultures in Nepal

A. THE INDIAN SCENE ACROSS THE BORDERS

As a result of the patient endeavours of archaeologists in India for over a hundred years, a rich ensemble of a sequence of cultures in India has come to light, though there are as yet many loose ends here and there. Apart from the discovery of extensive remains of the prehistoric Stone Age man in the form of old stone age tools, in two stages, followed by those of the neolithic civilization going back to the 4th millennium B.C., the sequence includes an assemblage of successive or partially overlapping cultures comprising the Harappa civilization (2300-1750 B.C.), multiple chalcolithic cultures, with regional characteristics, with common as well as mutually exclusive elements (2000-700 B.C.), spreading from Rajasthan to West Bengal with ramifications in certral and western India, multiple deposits of sophisticated and stylized hoards of copper weapons, of an as yet unknown chronology, a widespread megalithic culture of sorts (1000 B.C. to 1st century A.D.), besides the so-called cultural remains (1000-400 B.C.) of the Aryan settlers of the Ganga plains, distinguished by a *de luxe* ceramic were called the Painted Grey Ware. The last ushers in the early historical period towards its terminal phases, overlapping with a distinctive ceramic called the Northern Black Polished Ware (500-200 B.C.). The interrelationships between one and another of this rather vast assemblage, however remain, yet to be determined, as also their correspondence to or correlation with any firmly identifiable ethnological or linguistic groups.

The cultural scene in India would naturally be expected to show some close contacts with the neighbouring lands of Nepal, especially as such contacts have been proved between India and her neighbours in the north-west, Central Asia and even in the Far East, beyond the seas, helping to understand the cultural history of Nepal.

B. THE SCENE IN NEPAL

(*i*) *Prehistory*

In contrast, however, the earliest settlements in the Tarai of Nepal, as revealed by the limited excavations carried out so far do not indicate a date range before 600 B.C. in the *Tarai* region, and those in the central valley of Kathmandu do not take us before the 5th century A.D. It cannot, however, be inferred that the region was a vacuum before this date. The present lack of evidence would have to be set down to the paucity of work rather than of evidence.

Tradition has it that the valley was anciently a great lake, the waters of which were released through an opening cut by the sword of *Manjusri.* Apart from the allegorical and legendary and even anachronistic aspects of the matter, it can be stated that geology has confirmed this phenomenon. The valley emerged as dry and as a result of the impounded waters finding their way out of the valley through a deep and narrow gorge at Chobhar, cut by the very pressure of the waters, after struggling incessantly to find a way out for thousands of years. The great event took place, according to the calculation of the geologists, about 200,000 years ago.

So far not a single palaeolithic tool of the stone Age Man has been found in Nepal. If however, there was any human life in the area at the time in the prehistoric past, even in its uppermost and latest phase the traces thereof could be found either at the periphery of the lake or in the thick of its silty depsoits which can be clearly seen in the stratified deposits of the valley section, as in Switzerland. This underscores the need for a patient search in these deposits or in the cliff sections of gravel deposits in the river valleys in the *Tarai* or the terraces of mature rivers all over the country.

Toni Hagen has drawn our attention to the existence of numerous man-made and natural caves in the region of Thakkhola in the extreme north, where remains of the prehistoric man are likely to be found. Several other caves are known to explorers. All these still await the probing hand of the archaeologist. Professor Giuseppe Tucci has, in his report of exploration in Western Nepal, also indicated the sporadic finds of several archaeological remains, including stone-made chambers, stone or wooden posts, serving as memorials to the dead, reminiscent of a widely prevalent megalithic culture of an unknown cultural or chronological association except in so far as they recall the practice prevalent among some Nagas of Assam. The practice of erecting some kind of stone memorials, recalling menhirs, are even now prevalent among the Kirats in eastern Nepal, and must be the relics of an older practice.

The recent discovery of unmistakable megalithic remains in the neighbourhood of Kalimpong by the West Bengal Directorate of Archaeology raises fresh hopes of finding intermediate relic in the intermediate regions of Nepal as well, and linking them up with as in India as well as Tibet. The matter is of striking interest and needs much investigation as a problem in Nepalese archaeology.

The periodic and sporadic reports of the find of polished stone axes in the region of Panau to the north of Kathmandu and elsewhere in Nepal and Sikkim, and the recent haul of a large collection of neolithic tools from near Kalimpong (India) besides the occurrence of megalithic burials of an unknown cultural association in the same region (Kalimpong) have raised hopes for similar finds in the different and comparable horizons of Nepal.

That these polished axes had been used anciently as hoes for cultivation, by fixing them with leather thongs or ropes of some kind to the end of a stick to be operated manually is distantly echoed, conservatively, by the still prevalent Newari custom of hand cultivation in the Kathmandu valley by means of iron or steel spade with curved tang fixed at the end of wooden handles. The persistent practice may prove itself to be a relic of the neolithic times. The situation easily calls for intensive work in search of the missing trails of the Stone Age man as they seem likely to be found by patient exploration.

(ii) *The Beginnings of the Historical Period*

It is well-known that Lumbini, the birth place of the Buddha, is within the borders of Nepal. The spot is marked by an inscribed pillar of stone erected by Asoka in the 21st year of his reign. Buddha himself does not seem to have travelled into any other part of Nepal. This is borne out by the fact that neither Fahien nor Yuan Chwang, the two renowned Chinese pilgrims who came all the way from China on a pilgrimage to all places hallowed by their association with the Buddha, did not visit any other places except Lumbini and Kapilavastu in Nepal. Yuan Chwang, who visited the court of Harsha of Kanauj, has of course mentioned Amsuvarma as the contemporary ruler of Nepal.

The evidence of at least two hemispherical and earthen *stupas* at Pulchowk and Patan out of a group of five in the Lalitpur area is attributed by tradition to Asoka, and the one at Chabolhil is attributed to Charumati, daughter of Asoka. The truth of the matter can only be established by the spade. Though the *stupas* at

Swayambhu and Bodhnath are attributed by tradition to Tibetan workmanship at an unknown date, they could have come into existence only after the introduction of Buddhism in Tibet. Here again the help of the spade alone could tell the truth, or else the mystery will linger unchallenged. For the present, however, these constitute the only relics of an unknown age and may or may not fill the lacunae before the historically known Lichchhavis.

(*iii*) *Early History*

Literary records in the form of *Vāṃśāvalīs* of much later date than the history to which they relate wax eloquent about the Kiratas as the earliest rulers of Nepal. There are till now neither material remains nor any archaeological evidence of these folks, not to speak of any inscriptional records. Strangely enough, there is no reference to them in the entire range of the numerous inscriptions of the Lichchhavis, who are supposed to have been their successors. The inscriptions, however, repeatedly mention the levy of a tax to fight off the Mallas who had no doubt been a thorn in the side of the Lichchhavis, apart from recording a showdown between the Mallas and Manadeva, the first historical Lichchhavi king known. In these days of science which has made it possible to recognize and date cultural remains of the remotest date, for instance the complete history and civilization of the Sumerians of Iraq, going back to the end of the fourth millennium B.C., all traditional beliefs, regardless of their value must eventually be tested on the touchstone of objectivity. It has not yet been possible to build up even a complete and connected account of the Lichchhavis or Mallas, who are both known to *Manusmriti* and are mentioned in the oldest Buddhist literature as living in the days of the Buddha, in the area around Vaisali, in Bihar and Kusinara and Pawa, in Uttar Pradesh, India.

Even in regard to the Lichchhavis, though spoken of as a republican tribe living around Vaiśāli in the Muzaffarpur District of Bihar, there is no evidence, at least for the present, in the *Tarai*, though they are referred to in the coins of Chandragupta I who ruled from A. D. 320-330 and in the Allahabad Pillar Inscription of his son and successor, Samudragupta (330-375). In fact, the provenance of their inscriptions, which should indicate the extent of the territories under their control point to an area delimited by Dharmasthali in the north, Palanchok in the east, Gorkha in the west, and Lele in the south. The Lichchhavis used the same script as was employed by the Gupta emperors of India during what is known as the Golden Age of Indian history, and the Saka era, beginning in A.D. 78 . Their earliest dated inscription takes us back to the year A.D. 464 (386 Śaka era). The history of the country before this date is mostly a blank, as far as records are concerned, but for a few landmarks here and there.

Professor Tucci has indicated the immense potentialities of discovering more antiquarian remains, particularly in the west and north, that may go a long way towards filling up of the persistently gaping lacunae in the history and archaeology of Nepal.

(*iv*) *Later History, Antiquities and Monuments*

The framework of later history is simple, though there again one is confronted with lacunae which remain to be filled archaeologically, despite the circumstance that, we are on surer grounds than ever before.

The teeming multitudes of the antiquities that were produced by the arts and crafts of Nepal in the form of tottering or standing monuments of sorts and a plethora of images and sculptures bespeak the sympathy of the nation. The task on hand is to sort them out, arrange them chronologically and take steps for their preservation to enable detailed study, and reclaim the lost facets of the practical lives of the peoples through the corridors of time since the Muse of History is otherwise mute. The value of these relics in buiding up the complete history of the arts and architecture as of the religions they subserved, and the involved technology of quarrying, carving, carpentry and engineering is immense and hardly needs to be stressed.

Resume of the Archaeological Work in Nepal

(*i*) *Prehistoric Expedition*

Though as yet no substantial traces of the prehistoric man have been found in Nepal, the circumstance is to be attributed to the comparative paucity of work in the field. A brief and preliminary work was, however, undertaken by Dr. R.V. Joshi, Superintending Archaeologist, Archaeological Survey of India in 1961 in selected areas in the valleys of the Vishnumati and Bagmati, at the request of the H.M.G. and at the instance of the Indian Cooperation Mission. Though Dr. Joshi's work did not yield any positive tesults beyond recording the nature of the riverine deposits of gravel, it served at once to train the local personnel in the methodology of prehistoric field work and at once to indicate the scope and emphasize the need of more sustained work in the direction. A brief report of the work has been published in *Indian Archaeology* 1961-62 *A Review* and a fuller report is awaited. This work was the first of its kind in Nepal.

(*ii*) *Exploration and Excavation of Ancient Sites*

The cultural framework established by the archaeologists in India as indicated above, could well serve as a readymade guide for traces of cultural contact between Nepal and India since the earliest days. For the present, however, the backward thrust of the Nepalese culture in the *tarai* shows some obvious contacts in the region about the middle of the first millennium B.C. This was about the time of the Buddha at the earliest level of occupation in the area on the basis of the find of a somewhat later form of the distinctive ceramic ware called the Painted Grey Ware. It may be recalled that this ware has been provisionally recognized as the *de luxe* pottery of the Aryans who settled in the Ganga plains and is dated between 1,000 and 400 B.C. Nepal catches up with it at a stage slightly earlier than its contact with another equally distinctive but later ceramic ware called the Northern Black Polished Ware datable to *circa* 600-200 B.C.

The discovery in 1893 of the well-known Lumbini Pillar inscription of Asoka of the twenty first year of his reign by A. Fuehrer, a German archaeologist, then in the employ of the Government of India, was followed by the discovery in 1896 of the Nigali Sagar pillar with Asoka's inscription recording the enlargement by his orders of the *stupa* of Konakamuni, a previous Buddha, in the fourteenth year of his reign and a visit to inspect the works and personally worship the hallowed spot in the twenty-first year by Major Jasokaran Singh of Balarampur. These were epoch making discoveries as they focussed the attention of the world upon the land of the Buddha with an irresistible charm. Though not strictly in formal sense Asoka may go down in history as the first archaeologist of the subcontinent with an eye on the needs of posterity for having rendered yeoman's service to the history and culture of Nepal as the first Indian ever in the field of international cooperation in repairing or preserving indelible archaeological and historical remains and records for the benefit of the countless generations of the future.

Almost simultaneously the stump of a bare pillar alongside a *stupa* was found at Gotihawa in the same region. The unrecorded excavation of the *stupa* by Major Waddel, a British officer of the Indian Army, led to the discovery of bones, recognised as animal bones, without further attempt at any scientific examination of the material. The excavation in 1897 by W. Peppe of the *stupa* at Piprahawa on the borders of Nepal, containing the inscribed relics of the Buddha laid to rest by his Śākya brethren, at a distance of 9 miles from Lumbini, was yet another milestone that focussed the attention of scholars all the world over upon the region around Lumbini as being very crucial for the study of the early historical period in the subcontinent. Eventually these discoveries led to the excavation of the Nepalese site of Tilaurakot, near Taulihawa, in the Lumbini Anchal, at a distance of 19 miles (14 miles as the crow flies) to the west of Lumbini, in 1899, by P.C. Mukherjee, an Indian engineer, with the permission of the then Nepalese Government.

Though no positive evidence was found by Mukherjee to clinch the issue regarding the identification of the site of Kapilavastu, he tentatively identified the site, on the basis of the well-preserved nature of the site, the existence of the traces of a mud fortification and a protective moat around, and its tallying to an extent with the description left of it in relation to other sites in the neighbourhood by Yuan Chwang with Kapilavastu, the capital of the Śākyas, regardless of its divergence with the descriptions of the earlier Chinese pilgrim, Fahien. This was at once revolutionary and attractive, and the provisional identification was gratefully accepted by the Nepalese. It should be recorded in this context that the *stupa* to the east of site, which was also opened up by Mukherjee, did not yield any relic worthy of consideration. Nor was any specifically Buddhistic relic ever reported from this or the subsequent brief excavations at Chitradei by Mukherjee on the opposite bank of the Ban Ganga facing Tilaurakot.

At the same time Mukherjee excavated the base of the pillar at Lumbini, reclaimed the scanty remains of the brick-built *Maya Devi* temple, containing fifth century sculptural panel of the scene of Buddha's Nativity, and identified a few *stupa* like structures on the site, along with the remains of a monastic establishment besides the tank in which queen Maya Devi is supposed to have bathed herself before the birth of Buddha.

Mukherjee also carried out fairly extensive exploration in the area, bringing to light many ancient sites that urgently claim and await excavations. All this was remarkable achievement. Mukherjee's book on the work entitled *'A Report on a Tour of Exploration of the Antiquities in the Tarai, Nepal'*, Calcutta, 1901, is a veritable mine of information and the first publication of its kind in respect of Nepal, published by the Archaeological Survey of India.

These important discoveries were followed by large-scale clearance operations around the pillar and temple in *Lumbini,* after a long gap of nearly 35 years, in 1933-34, at the enlightened instance of His late Highness Field Marshall Kaiser Samsher Rana. These works resulted in the exposure of an extensive area to the south-west of the pillar, revealing straggling remains of monasteries and *stupas*, and a host of diverse antiquities, including sculptures, moulded bricks, coins, and of course pottery that span an extensive range of time from *circa* 6th century B.C. to 9th century A.D.

A few sherds of the Painted Grey Ware, found in the exposed trenches and on the surface, indicate the ancient moorings of the site.

The first scientific excavation in Nepal was, however, carried out by Shrimati D. Mitra, a senior officer of the Archaeological Survey of India, in a joint undertaking with the Department of Archaeology, under a scheme sponsored by the Indian Cooperation Mission, in 1961, when she excavated a trench at Tilaurakot the old site first brought to light by Mukherjee. She also exposed partially the base of the pillar at Lumbini and explored a large number of sites to the west of Lumbini. Shrimati Mitra's report of her work entitled '*Excavations at Tilaurakot and Kodan and Exploration in Districts Bhairhwa and Taulihawa*' is in the press. This will form the first large and exhaustive work on the subject.

Subsequently again the site was excavated by Shri T.N. Mishra, Exploration and Excavation officer of the H. M. G., Department of Archaeology, in 1966 and 1967 (under the general guidance of the author), and briefly by a Japanese team of the Rhisso University of Tokyo under the leadership of Professor Kuba, in 1967, under a five-year agreement with the H.M.G.

The excavations by the Indian and Nepalese agencies have revealed traces of a habitation on the site that would easily go back to the sixth century B.C., if not still earlier, on the basis of the find of somewhat degenerate specimens of the well dated Aryan ceramic, called the Painted Grey Ware, showing a time lag, and the circumstantial evidence of the association of the region generally with Buddha who flourished in the sixth century B.C. To an extent this date has been indicated by the carbon date of a charcoal specimen from the site, studied by the Tata Institute of Fundamental Research, Bombay, working out to *circa* 400 B.C. More evidence is at once awaited and called for to clinch the issue. The inferences for the present are at best tentative.

Dr. S. B. Deo in his capacity as Colombo Plan Prefessor of Ancient Indian Culture at the Tribhuvan University, provided by the Indian Cooperation Mission, carried out two excavations at Hadigaon and Lajimpat, in Kathmandu, in the summer of 1965, yielding evidence of habitation reaching back to the Lichchhavi period at the earliest. Dr. Deo had already carried out excavations at Banjarahi and Paisia, in the region of Lumbini, in the summer of 1964, and undertook explorations in the region to the east of Lumbini, left untouched by Shrimati D. Mitra, and brought to light a large number of archaeological sites in the area.

These excavations by Deo were also joint undertakings of the Indian Cooperation Mission and the Department of Archaeology, and the reports in two volumes are in the press and will be out before long.

The excavations at Banjarahi showed two periods of occupation, the earlier of which was associated and characterized by the Painted Grey Ware, which overlapped with another distinctive ceramic designated as the Northern Black Polished Ware with a date range of 600-200 B.C. The earliest occupation of the site could therefore be assigned to the sixth century B.C., if not still earlier. The excavations at Banjarahi by Deo revealed a complex of brick-built temples, dating back to the medieval period.

Likewise Shrimati D. Mitra's excavation at Kodan in 1961, about 3 miles to the south of Tilaurakot, carried out in the hope of exposing a complex of *stupas*, had resulted in the partial exposure of a complex of medieval temples (8th century), with no relevance whatsover to Buddhism, for the central shrine is clearly a Siva temple as revealed by the broken remnant of a *linga* in the sanctum.

Early in 1966, the exploration and excavation branch of the H.M.G., Department of Archaeology undertook under the author's guidance the first excavations by an all Nepal team at Dhum Varahi, on the northern outskirts of Kathmandu, and found the remains of a late Lichchhavi occupation on the site, comprising among others numerous specimens of terracotta art including, moulds of artistic scenes, inscribed seals, vessels serving as measures of liquids in terms of 5 *prasthas* (pathis), and uniquely the figure of a terracotta camel, dating back to about 7th century A.D.

(*iii*) *Conservation of Ancient Monuments and Remains*

(a) Repairs to Monuments

The machinery of conservation of ancient monuments is vested in the *Guthi Jirnnoddhar Tatha Prachin Smarak Samrakshan Samiti* (Committee for the preservation of Ancient Monuments) of the *Guthi Samsthan*. A large number of ancient monuments has been taken up for conservation during the last two years by this body functioning under the chairmanship of the Director of Archaeology. The funds are provided entirely by the *Guthi Samsthan* (Religious Endowments).

(b) Chemical Conservation

The initial work of the chemical conservation of the then fading and almost obscured murals in the Picture Gallery Museum at Bhaktapur was undertaken and completed during 1965-66 through an officer of the Chemical Branch of the Archaeological Survey of India at the instance of the Indian Cooperation Mission. Simultaneously two young Nepalese chemists of the Department were trained in the rudiments of the complex and variegated work of chemical conservation in general. At the same time similar work of clearing and preserving the colourful murals at the Kumari Ghar was also commenced by the Indian chemist with the help of his Nepalese colleagues. Subsequent work by the trained chemists working on their own at the Kumari Ghar and Hanuman Dhoka have won them laurels.

(iv) Inscriptions and Coins

The Department has been collecting estampages of inscriptions and copies of copper plate grants and inscriptions, in various languages, though predominantly in Sanskrit, and in the Brāhmi and Devanāgari scripts in their many ramifications, as these form a very substantial record for reconstructing the history of Nepal. The work is being attended to mainly by the two epigraphists in the employ of the Department. Among the scholars who have made substantial contributions in this direction special mention may be made of C. Bendall (Great Britain), Sylvain Levi (France), Bhagwan Lal Indraji (India), Buehler (Germany), R. Gnoli (Italy) and groups of Nepalese scholars, including those belonging to the *Itihāsa Samśodhana Maṇḍal*, besides Dr. D. R. Regmi, Yogi Narahari Nath, Shri Hemraj Sakya and Shri Sankarman Rajbanshi (the last two being officers of the Department).

The earliest inscriptional records in the *tarai* are the pillar inscriptions of Asoka at Lumbini and Nigali Sagar, dating back to the middle of the third century B. C. But the earliest inscription in the Kathmandu valley is the Changu Narayan inscription of Manadeva dated to 384 *Samvat* (A. D. 466). As to coins, the earliest ones discovered so far comprise the punch-marked coins of copper found in the excavations at Tilaurakot followed by the coins of the Pañchāla Kings (2nd century B.C.) and of the Kushans (1st 2nd centuries A.D.). The earliest coins found in the Kathmandu valley are the Mananka coins of Manadeva, dated to 5th century A.D.

The Numismatist of the Department who is currently in charge of the coin museum at Kathmandu had his training at the Banaras Hindu University.

The facts that coins receive specialised attention from the Department has been mentioned in connexion with museums elsewhere in these pages.

(v) Iconographical and Architectural Survey

One of the most interesting works to be undertaken in the field of archaeology in recent years was the comprehensive survey of Nepalese sculptures in the Kathmandu valley, in stone, wood and bronze, made by Shri K. Deva, now Director of the School of Archaeology in the Archaeological Survey of India, under the joint auspices of the H.M.G. and the Indian Cooperation Mission, in 1963. The report is under preparation.

More recently a beginning has been made in making a comprehensive survey of sculptures and architectural remains with an eye on their preservation and study.

The art of Nepal has engaged the attention of scholars from the very beginning of Nepal's contacts with scholars from outside the borders, but it is only now that the study is gaining in momentum, as the contacts and mutual exchanges have become closer. It was Professor Stella Kramarisch who first wrote a comprehensive though inadequate book on the '*Art of Nepal*' (1964). This was followed by the Department's own publication of a catalogue entitled '*Nepalese Art*' (1966). Objects of art from Nepal have been exhibited in recent years over a large part of the globe including several countries in Europe and Asia under the auspices of the Department and a roving exhibition from Nepal will be shortly on display at the International Exhibition of Art in Mexico to coincide with the forthcoming (19th) Olympic Games.

(vi) Museums and the control of traffic in Antiquities

The Department has presently seven museums under its control, namely the Nepal Museum and the Coin Museum at Kathmandu, the Archaeological Garden-cum-Museum and the Museum of Excavated Antiquities at Patan, the Picture Gallery and Woodworks Museum at Bhaktapur, and the Archaeological Site Museum at Taulihawa (Tilaurakot-Kapilavastu). Of these the Nepal Museum, which is the oldest museum in Nepal and also the national museum and covers several other aspects besides archaeology, was founded in 1928. The first two successive keepers of the museum were Shri S. N. Sen and Shri Benode Bihary Bhattacharya, respectively. These museologists, both from India, contributed considerably to the museum movement in Nepal in general and to the building up of the nucleus collection of what has now become the National Museum.

It is comforting to record that the export of antiquities from Nepal is prohibited by the law of the land and the control of and vigilance over the movement of the antiquities has been presently entrusted to the authorites of the National Museum of Nepal.

(vii) Research and Publications

The reports of the various works carried out by Indian archaeologists are mostly ready, and some are in the last stages of printing in the press.

The Department itself has started its own bilingual journal entitled *Prachin Nepal* (*Ancient Nepal*), that comes out once in three months since October '67. Three issues have already come out and the fourth is in the press.

One of its attractive publications is a catalogue of Nepalese art objects entitled '*Nepalese Art.*' It was prepared on the eve of the organization of the roving exhibition of Nepalese art objects, first held in Paris, in October 1966, that has been going round the world during the last two years.

The Department has also published four books on the palaeography of the different scripts used in Nepal, besides a list of inscriptions collected from Bhaktapur, with the essential parts of the inscriptions adequately abbreviated.

(viii) Organizational, Training and Miscellaneous Works

One of the first archaeologists to be formally invited by H.M.G. in recent times, in 1961, to suggest ways and means for the proper organization of the Department was Shri A. Ghosh, then Director General of Archaeology in India, under the auspices of the Indian Cooperation Mission. Shri Ghosh's visit paved the way for (a) the first prehistoric expedition in the valley by Dr. R. V. Joshi (1961), (b) excavations at Lumbini and Tilaurakot by Shrimati D. Mitra and the exploration of the region to the east of Lumbini (1961), (c) the iconographical survey of the sculptures of Nepal under Shri K. Deva, (d) initiation of chemical conservation in Nepal, (e) training of the entire technical staff of the Department comprising a draftsman, a surveyor, an engineering officer for archaeological conservation, an Egigraphist and an iconographist, respectively, in the different lines of their work at the various relevant offices of the Archaeological Survey of India, besides, (f) the supply of a large number of books by the Indian cooperation Mission towards building up the essential nucleus of a research library of the

Department. Shri Ghosh also submitted a general organization and developmental plan for the Department, which has been gradually implementing.

In addition to the training of technical staff and officers mentioned above, an officer of the Survey has successfully undergone the (nearly) two-year Diploma course in Archaeology at the School of Archaeology of the Archaeological Survey of India, and three of the museologists of the Department have received training at different time in the course of Museology at the Department of Museology at the Baroda University under a Colombo Plan Scheme of scholarships offered by the Indian Cooperation Mission. This trained personnel represents the present and future hope and mainstay of the Department's manifold activities that are under way.

(ix) Archaeological Advisers

The Department also secured the services of an Unesco Adviser for Archaeology for a year in 1964-65, and, on the expiry of his term, a senior officer of the Archaeological Survey of India was appointed under the Colombo Plan of the Indian Cooperation Mission to work as Adviser to H.M.G. for Archaeology, in April 1966. The present adviser has been throughout associated actively with all aspects of the Department's work, comprising exploration and excavation, conservation of ancient monuments, preparation of a catalogue of Nepalese Art, publication of the Department's own Bulletin entitled *Ancient Nepal*, collection of data on monuments and sculptures, and preparation of excavation and technical reports, besides undertaking research on diverse topics, and the continued training of technical hands in their respective fields during the last two and a half years.

In recent months the Department has also been enlisting in addition the services of short term experts on museums, conservation of monuments, cultural tourism and chemical conservation etc. from the Unesco.

(x) Development of Lumbini

It is admitted on all hands that the world-famous site of Lumbini with the temple of Maya Devi, ruins of the monasteries and *stupas* that once hummed with activity in the vicinity of the hallowed spot of the birth of Buddha, in the midst of what was then a garden, with the ancient village not very far removed from the site, would lend itself to considerable improvement towards revival of its ancient glories.

The 6 mile long motorable road that connects Lumbini with Kakrahawa on the Indian border, leading on to Naugarh Rly. Station in District Basti, Uttar Pradesh, was built by India in 1956, and made over to the H.M.G. in 1958. It was then and is even now an essential means of communication used by large numbers of pilgrims and tourists visiting the site from the Indian side.

Conclusion

It would be clear to see that though much has already been achieved by the young Department of Archaeology, during the very short time of its existence, a great deal remains yet to be done. The task lying ahead of us is simply enormous and staggering by its very nature. It would be at once the envy and pride of even the most well-organized and advanced archaeological institution in any part of the world, for the challenge posed by the task and its myriad facetted problems is irresistible.

Apart from the Nepalese themselves, many hands from the different countries of Asia and Europe, including, though on a much smaller scale, some from the United States also, have joined in the none too large endeavour to uncover the various aspects of Nepalese history and culture.

Discovery of Lithic Artifacts in Jammu Area

by G. C. MOHAPATRA and HARI MOHAN SAROJ

The region of Jammu was a *terra incognita* as regards prehistoric cultures till a press report in August 1966 announced the discovery of a few Sohanian pebble-tool sites from the Ravi valley in the Kathua district[1]. Previously from Kangra district in Himachal Pradesh adjoining Jammu, not only similar pebble tools but also a large number of small flake-tools and Neolithic polished stone celts had been discovered which revealed a fairly coherent picture of the development of lithic cultures in that region[2]. The exciting new discovery from the Ravi valley provided a very encouraging lead to search for the extensions of these prehistoric cultures in the region of Jammu, the low hilly areas of which present almost identical physiographical and geological features as that of the Kangra district. This note presents the first set of results of the field investigations carried out by the junior author in connection with a research scheme "Lithic Industries of Jammu" conducted under the supervision of the senior author.

Explorations in the valley of the Ravi and its tributaries like the Ujh, the Tarnah, the Ben and the Basantar ; and the Tawi, a tributary of the Chenab, have yielded artifacts of two lithic industries namely, the Early Sohan and the industry of the small flake-tools. The former industry occurs on high river terraces at Nagrota on the Tawi (Dist. Jammu), Kuta on the Ben (Dist. Kathua), Drui on the Basantar (Dist. Jammu), Dyalachak on the Tarnah (Dist. Kathua) and Jandore on the Ravi (Dist. Kathua), whereas the latter industry was found also on the terraces at Rajbagh on the Ujh (Dist. Kathua) and along with the former at Kuta and Dyalachak.

The Sohanian pebble-tools display the traditional technique and typology as are peculiar to this culture. But one specimen, a unifacial pebble-tool, is exceptionally interesting (Pl. I, fig. 5), Its pick-like form is a distinct departure from the chopper-choppig tool typology. All the flakes removed, from one face of the elongated flat pebble, were primarily aimed at reducing the thickness of the edges and one end of the pebble to a thin tip like that of a handaxe. The other end retains the whole of the pebble cortex as seen on many of the smooth-pebble-butted handaxes of the peninsular variety. Another feature, which is alien to the Shohanian tradition, is the multi-directional flaking technique. The flakes which have been struck off from both margins, bottom upward, of one surface only, ultimately converge at the tip. This extensive flaking covering nearly three fourth of the total area of one surface has produced a sharp working-edge around more than half of the periphery of the pebble and has made the tool pyriform. Although a hundred percent pebble-tool, this specimen is distinct from the Sohanian pebble-tools due to the above typo-technological peculiarities. Those who are acquainted with the lithic cultures of the north western part of the Indian subcontinent will not fail to appreciate the significance of this specimen because howsoever faint, this provides a clue which when carefully followed might help us in settling the long drawn controversy about the presence of handaxe-cleaver culture in this part and its relationship with the Sohanian.

The small flake-tools prepared out of the siliceous raw materials display advanced techniques as are found in the Middle Stone Age industries of India. The flakes, usually struck from the prepared cores, have been dressed into various types of scrapers. There are a few small and flat chert pebbles also dressed into scrapers which look like miniature pebble choppers due to the unifacial and one directional flaking so typical of the Sohanian. The character of this industry in Jammu compares well with that of the small flake-tool industry found in Kangra district [3]. It is too premature to comment on its exact relationship with the peninsular lithic culture complex.

The results of this preliminary field investigations in Jammu when interpolated into the data previously obtained from Kangra, combine these two regions into one cultural unit and emphasise its vast potentiality for future fruitful research.

NOTES

[1] *The Tribune*, daily, Ambala, 14th August, 1966.

[2] M. R. Sahani, & G. C. Mohapatra, ' The First Record of Small Flake-Tools and Polished Stone Celts in Kangra District, E. Punjab ', *Current Science*, March 20, 1964, vol. 33, no. 6, pp. 178-180.

[3] G. C. Mohapatra, 'Preliminary Report of the Exploration and Excavation of Stone Age Sites in E. Punjab ', *Bulletin of the Deccan College Research Institute*, *Poona*, Vol. 25, p. 229.

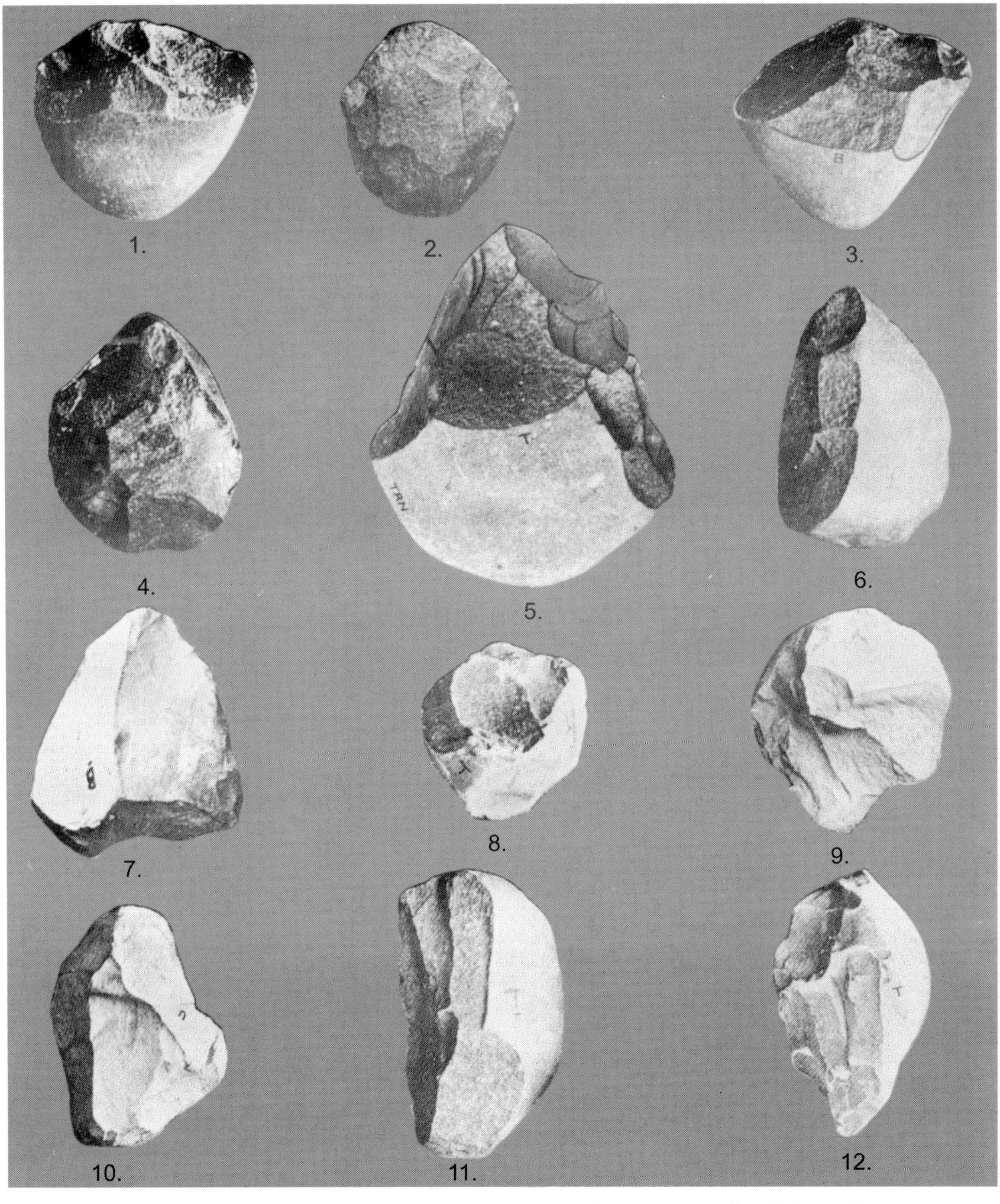

Lithic artifacts from Jammu : No. 1-6 Early Sohan; 7-12 smaller flake tools.

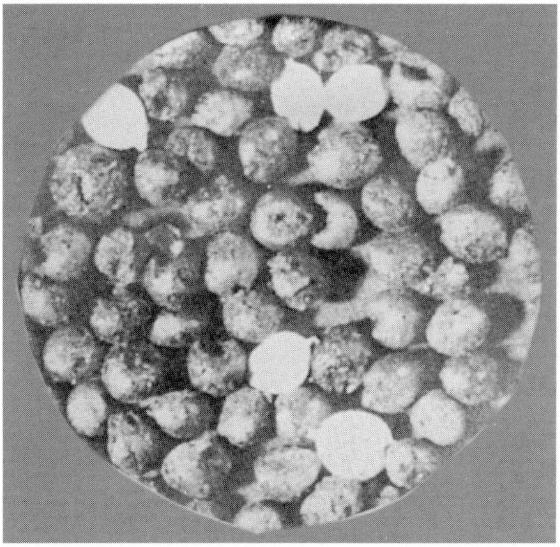

A. 1 Carbonised grains of *Sorghum* sp. x 4 from Bhatkuli. The white seeds are of modern *Sorghum* sp.

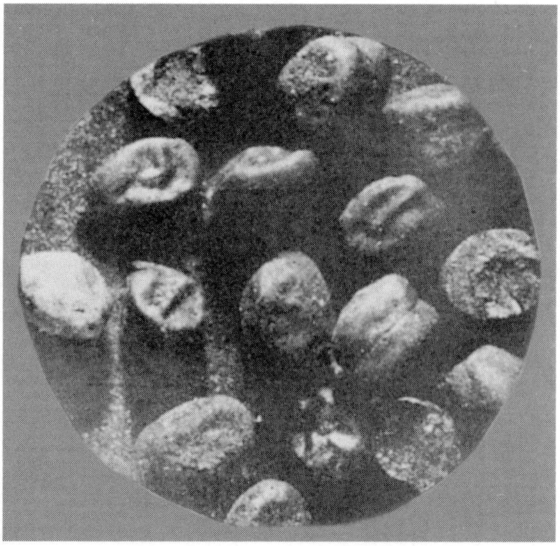

A. 2 Carbonised seeds of *Cicer arietinum* x 2.

B. Fossil-bones from a pit on the Purna, western Maharashtra.

Regional Variations in the Indian Middle Stone Age Culture with Special Reference to Nalgonda in Andhra Pradesh

by S.N. RAO

The Indian Middle Stone Age as a separate cultural entity characterised by a large group of diminutive flake tools has been fairly well established after the discovery of the Nevasian Industry by Sankalia in 1954 in a distinctly stratified horizon. This culture occupies the intermediate position which was preceded by the Early Stone Age and succeeded by the Late Stone Age. Broadly it covers the period from the end of Middle Pleistocene and continues in Upper Pleistocene including the earlier part of Holocene. Since the discovery of the Nevasian culture a number of sites showing similar cultural evidence have been reported from the sub-continent. [1].

Sankalia observes that "in a vast country like India there are bound to be regional variations (in the Middle Stone Age Culture) attributable to ecological, geographical and other factors". So, keeping this point in view, an attempt is made here to bring into focus the diversities that are evident in the industries of the Middle Stone Age culture from various regions in India in general and Nalgonda in particular.

The archaeological record of the Indian Early Stone Age period stretching over a great span of time shows a general uniformity of method of manufacture and form of stone implements in time and space.

The succeeding Middle Stone Age heralded a new phase of cultural trend resulting in several regional manifestations and yet all displaying certain dominant common cultural traits.

There was general switch-over in the choice of raw material for obtaining flake tools during this period, preferring such fine-grained silicious minerals like chert, jasper, agate and chalcedony as is evident in the industries from Andhra (Asifabad) [2], Maharashtra (Nevasa) [3], Rajasthan [4], Madhya Pradesh (Narmada Valley) [5], Northern Bundelkhand [6] and Orissa [7]. That the flake tools were made not only on silicious materials but the same quartzite of fine-grained variety was continued to be chiefly favoured in this period as in the Early Stone Age is clear from the industries of such sites as Kurnool [8], Cuddapah [9], Chittur [10] in Andhra, Sirsa Valley in the East Punjab, and Upper Soan in Pakistan [11].

A significant achievement in this phase was the technological progress explicit in the predominance of the production of flakes and flake-blades from cores previously prepared to get tools of desired shape and size, a technique which was economical both of labour and of raw material. The preparation of either core or striking platform or both can be observed in these industries. Fluted core method was also prevalent to some extent. At the same time most of the flakes were infact obtained from cores without previous preparation or by "plain" flaking technique. These stone techniques were employed either individually or together at different sites. In the industries of Nevasa and Kurnool, Rajasthan,

Narmada Valley, Northern Bundelkhand and the Upper Soan a few flakes and cores (increasingly in the Upper Soan 'B') show previous preparation of striking platform and of core recalling the Levallois technique. The knowledge of previous preparation of core and striking platform is unknown in the industries of some areas like Orissa and the plain flaking cylinder hammer technique was continued throughout. Though rare, the fluted core method was evidently used for the manufacture of blades along with the above mentioned stone techniques. This feature is seen in the Middle Stone Age industries of Damoh Area [12], in Madhya Pradesh and Northern Bundelkhand, some of them occurring in the stratified deposits and others from the factory sites.

Typologically the tools of the Middle Stone Age culture show some distinct diversities. Some characteristic tool types like scraper, borer and point repeatedly appear in all the industries. Biface or handaxe,cleaver and chopper of diminished size, the typical tool types of the Early Stone Age industries of the areas like Chittur (Andhra) Rajasthan, Northern Bundelkhand and Upper Soan. The occurrence of burin as a definite tool type of this culture is a matter of controversy though they are reported from Orissa and the Narmada Valley.

So far as the size of the tools are concerned those of Kurnool, Rajasthan, Northern Bundelkhand, Sirsa Valley and Upper Soan A are comparatively larger than the diminutive artifacts of other regions.

The Middle Stone Age culture in most of the regions led to the development of the Late Stone Age culture of microlithic facies whereas in Kurnool and Chittur in Andhra it gave rise to "blade and burin industry", typical of the European Upper Palaeolithic traditions.

In Nalgonda district [13] of Andhra Pradesh, where I carried out a systematic survey for the evidence of prehistoric cultures from 1962 to'65, the Middle Stone Age culture shows the following industrial elements and variations.

Stratigraphically the *in situ* implements of this industry occupy the gravel II of the second aggradational cycle, succeeding the Early Stone Age industry of the basal or first gravel horizon. A bulk of the artifacts are found in an unrolled condition at the factory site of Ramatirthampaya.

This industry comprising 589 artifacts is broadly classified into two groups based on the following criteria:

(A) the technique

(B) the size of the artifacts, and

(C) the raw material.

The group I implements are characterised by the widespread use of 'plain" flaking cylinder hammer technique and none of the flakes show the evidence of previous preparation either of striking platform or of upper surface. Another distinguishing feature of this group is the size of the tools which are relatively larger than their counterparts in group II. Lastly, they are exclusively made on medium-grained quartzite of various shades.

Flakes and flake-blades of group II are distinguished by the extensive use of 'prepared' core technique, the backs of which generally retain a series of flat and convergent flake scars. Knowledge of fluted core technique is obvious on the Middle Stone Age industry of Nalgonda as a few blades and fluted cores are found in association with the flakes of this industry at the workshop at Ramatirthampaya. They are made of the same material, that is, fine-grained quartzite of grey colour and are in the same physical condition as the rest of the artifacts which are stained to deep brown colour as they lay on brown sandy soil. In contrast to the implements of group I, those of group II are marked by their diminished size.

The implements of both the groups exhibit retouch and marks of use in different regions.

They are placed into two divisions according to the shape and the character of the working edge with no attempt at suggestion as to their use [14].

A. Single tools

B. Multiple tools

The tool types in both the groups are identical and these are as follows:

Single tools: 1. straight edge, single or double, 2. convex edge, 3. concavo-convex edge, 4. notched, 5. pointed and 6. discoidal.

Multiple tools: In this, a combination of any two types of working edges, as mentioned above, can be found on a single specimen to serve dual function.

These tools are comparable with their counterparts in the industries of other areas bearing such functional terms like scraper, borer, point and scraper-cum-borer.

The biface, cleaver and burin types are lacking in this industry. This is replaced by the Late Stone Age of non-geometric microlithic facies.

Thus the Middle Stone Age industry of Nalgonda, while basically showing a common cultural pattern, essentially differs from the industries of some regions and closely corresponds with some others in certain industrial elements.

The continued dependence on quartzite as raw material as well as the survival of chopper, hand-axe and cleaver types in this culture as in the Early Stone Age indicate a relationship between the two cultures. The variation in the choice of the raw material was primarily due to non-availability of silicious minerals in the areas of quartzite using industries.

The progressive technological change revealed in the tool equipment of the Middle Stone Age folk is at best a reflection of the adaption to the changed environment and the variations in this regard were presumably conditioned by local genius and relative isolation of each group of people from the mainstream of cultural contacts.

The survival of old tool types in some of the Middle Stone Age industries even at a time where there were substitute types, is largely attributable to the conservative attitude of the people who were reluctant to give up old methods and forms that had been in vogue for centuries.

NOTES

[1] H. D. Sankalia, 'Middle Stone Age Cultures in India and Pakisan', *Science*, 1965, 365-375.

[2] S. N. Rao, 'A Middle Stone Age Industry at Asifabad', *Bull. Dec. Col. Res. Inst.* XXV, 1966, 199-206.

[3] H. D. Sankalia, *et al.*, *From History to Prehistory at Nevasa*, Poona, 1960.

[4] V. N. Misra, *The Stone Age Cultures of Rajputana*, Ph.D. Thesis. Poona University, 1961.

[5] H. D. Sankalia, *Prehistory and Protohistory in India and Pakistan*, Bombay, 1962.

[6] R. Singh, *Palaeolithic Industries of Northern Bundelkhand*, Ph.D. Thesis. Poona University, 1965.

[7] G. C. Mohapatra, *Stone Age Cultures ofOrissa*, Poona, 1962.

[8] N. Isaac, *The Stone Age Cultures of Kurnool*, Ph.D. Thesis. Poona University, 1960.

[9] Information from Sri K. Timma Reddi who is at present working on the Stone Age sequence of Cuddapah District.

[10] M. L. K. Murty, *Stone Age Cultures of Chittur District*, Ph.D. Thesis, Poona University, 1966.

[11] T. T. Paterson, and H. J. H. Drummond, *Soan, the Palaeolithic of Pakistan*, 1962.

[12] R. V. Joshi, 'Stone Age Industries of the Damoh Area', *Ancient India*, No. 17, 1960, 5-36.

[13] S. N. Rao, *Stone Age Cultures of Nalgonda District*, Ph.D. Thesis. Poona University, 1966.

[14] T. T. Paterson, 'Palaeolithic Succession in England', *P.P.S.* VII, 1937, 93.

Some New Fossil Discoveries from Western Maharashtra, India

by S. N. RAJAGURU

During the last four years the author had an opportunity to explore some parts of the upper reaches of the Godavari, the Bhima and the Krishna rivers in western Maharashtra. On many of his field trips he was fortunate to have the company of eminent scholars like Prof. H.D. Sankalia, Dr. G.G. Mujumdar, Dr. Z.D. Ansari and Dr. Mrs. Corvinus of the Deccan College, Poona. They have the lion's share in these discoveries. The fossils collected from the Dam sites would not have seen the light of the day if the authorities in charge would not have taken interest in our work and provided the necessary facilities. The main purpose of writing this note is to bring all these discoveries in a more coherent way and to attempt to interpret the data collected.

After the initial discoveries of animal fossil bones in the alluvial deposits of the Godavari and the Krishna by geologists and palaeontologists like Twemlow, Cook, Pilgrim (1905) and others, these deposits were mostly dated to the Pleistocene period. The fossil bones discovered by them belonged to species like *Elephas Namadicus*, *Bos Namadicus*, *Hippopotamus palaeinducus*, *Equus Namadicus* etc. Later on Sankalia (1943-1964) systematically studied the alluvial deposits of various streams in the W. Maharashtra and his findings of the archaeological materials in association with *in situ* fossil bones especially that of *Bos Namadicus* at Kalegaon in the Godavari could help him in sub-dividing Stone Age cultures and also Pleistocene period itself. During this period the various exposed tool bearing deposits in association with the fossils mentioned above were dated to Middle Pleistocene. Later on after the detailed study of the fossils from the older alluvium of the Narmada by Khatri (1962) and on comparative analysis he thought that *Bos Namadicus*, found in association with Middle Stone Age tools in the Godavari, is a late survival of the Middle Pleistocene times and the dating of the archaeological material goes to Upper Pleistocene. Thus two main aggradational and erosional cycles more or less got established in many of the streams of Maharashtra and the Early Stone Age industry belonging to 1st aggradational cycle and the Middle Stone Age industry belonging to the 2nd aggradational cycle were dated to Late Middle Pleistocene and Upper Pleistocene respectively. Recently Joshi (1966) found a jaw of *Bos Namadicus* along with large number of very neatly worked handaxes, cleavers, etc., in a sandy pebbly gravel of the Godavari near Gangapur in Dist. Nasik and he dated the Early Stone Age industry of Gangapur to the Middle Pleistocene.

The new fossil discoveries are mainly from the Pleistocene deposits of the Godavari (near Paithan), the Mula (near Baregaon Nandur) in Dist. Ahmednagar, the Purna (near Yeldari) in Dist. Parbhani, the Ghod (near Kalamb and Chandoli) and the Mula-Mutha (near Bhivari) in Dist. Poona. All these sites, excepting Chandoli, have yielded *in situ* fossil bones in the Pleistocene deposits. The dam excavations at Paithan, Rahuri and Yeldari provided us an excellent opportunity to collect materials from the freshly exposed, uncontaminated sedimentary horizons. The exact location of the site, its geological and archaeological context and the possible identification of the fossil species etc., have been given below.

1. R. Godavari at Paithan

On the right bank of the Godavari, a fossil bone along with a few Middle Stone Age tools was collected from a sandy pebbly gravel exposed during the excavation for a dam construction. The location of the deposit was about 1km. away from the present Rt. bank of the stream and was 7m. above the present bed level of the stream. The alluvium buried below the modern bed is between 3 & 6 m. There is a clear cut evidence of the shifting of the Godavari from south to north. The fossil bone belongs to the Sp. *Bos*. The author feels that the fossils discovered by earlier workers at Paithan should also belong to Middle Stone Age.

2. R. Mula at Baregaon Nandur

Site A—A huge cut off trench on the right bank of the Mula was taken for the construction of a dam. The trench had exposed an alluvium, about 40 m. deep and 800 m. laterally extended from the right bank. The upper part of the alluvium (i. e. first 10 m. from the surface) was comparatively fine grained and was essentially sandy and silty while the lower part was coarse grained and contained large number of lenticular bodies of pebbly and bouldery conglomerates. Two unrolled fossil bones and fragmentary pieces of fossil wood (semi-carbonized) were collected *in-situ* from the sandy pebbly or bouldery gravels generally occuring 10 m. below the present bed level of the Mula. All these fossils occurred in a lateral distance of about 200 m. No cultural material was found in association with these fossils. Only in the top-most portion of the alluvium (15 m. above the level of fossil bearing stratum) a few Middle Stone Age tools were noticed. In the Mula also there is a clear cut evidence of shifting of the course of the stream from south to north. The identification of fossils is as follows:

(a) A left horizontal ramus of mandible with some teeth of *Bos Namadicus* Falconer.

(b) A horn of *Bubalus bubalis linnaeus*.

(c) The wood pieces resemble *Terminalia Arjuna* in anotomical characters. These semi-carbonized samples have been dated by C-14 method to about 33,000 yrs. B.P.

Site B—In the spill-way excavation on the left bank of the Mula two more fossil bones were found in the sandy pebbly gravel. Culturally only one genuine Middle Stone Age flake on chert was found in the same gravel horizon which occurred 3 m. below the present bed level of the Mula. The fossil identification is :

(a) Jaw of *Bos namadicus* with a few teeth.

(b) Fragmentary pieces of a tusk of *Elephas*.

The Mula meanders quite widely in this area and from the geomorphological evidence it appears that the pre-depositional channel of the Mula was about 14 to 17 m. below the present bed level and the shifting towards north has occurred in comparatively recent times. The present course of the Mula has exposed only 12-15 m. of the alluvium and has yielded good number of Middle Stone Age tools near Baregaon Nandur.

3. R. Purna at Yeldari

During the dam construction on the Purna, a tributary of the Godavari, a pit, 20 m. deep and 8 m. wide (longitudinal extent unknown) filled with alluvium, was found in the otherwise rocky bed of the Purna. This pit, probably a local gorge formed naturally, served as a natural pit-fall for the animals. We could collect large number of practically unrolled bones of an elephant along with some rolled bones of other species in the basal coarser gravel of the pit (Plate IIB). Unfortunately, no archaeological material was found in association with these bones.

These bones have been identified as follows:

(a) Fragment of cheek tooth of *Stegodon Insignis* Falconer and *Cautley*.

(b) Fragment of cheek tooth of *Elephas hysudricus* Falconer and *Cautley*.

(c) Fragments of mandible, distal fragment of left humerus, of tibia, proximal fragment of left humerus and large fragments of tusk of an *Elephas*. (Probably all these and others unidentified bones belong to one elephant).

(d) Distal fragment of right femur of *Bos*.

4. R, Ghod at Kalamb and Chandoli

Both these places are situated about 64 km. NE of Poona, on the left and right banks of the Ghod respectively, the latter place is little downstream of the earlier one. At Kalamb an *in-situ* fossil shoulder bone probably of *Elephas hysudricus* was recovered from a very well cemented sandy pebbly gravel exposed in the bed of a stream. The gravel rests directly on a basaltic rock and is overlain by finer sands and red brown kankary silt. No cultural material was found in association with the fossil bone. While at Chandoli a large number of fragmentary pieces of tusk, along with a few Middle Stone Age tools, were collected from a talus deposit accumulated at the foot of the cliff composed of ancient alluvium. The maximum basal girth of one of the largest and intact piece of tusk came to about 65 cm. and the total weight of all the pieces was found to be 63 kg. The average basal girth of the tusk of a modern Indian elephant is about 50 cm., while it had been found to be about 56 cm. in the case of *Elephas namadicus* found in the ancient alluvium of the Godavari. From all these considerations the tusk found at Chandoli appears to belong to some extinct species of an elephant.

5. R. Mula-Mutha at Bhivari.

About 32 km. east of Poona, a fragmentary bone of *Bos* and a distal fragment of a right radius of a *Bos* were found in a lenticular patch of a sandy pebbly gravel occurring in the yellow brown kankary silt which had formed a cliff on the left bank of the stream. The gravel was 5 m. above the bed level of the stream. A few Middle Stone Age tools were found in association with these bones. Besides these *in-situ* fossil bones, a large number of bones have been collected from the modern bed of the Pravara at Nevasa and a few from the Godavari, Ghod and the Bhima proper. The river Krishna has so far not yielded any fossil bones. All these loose fossil bones have been excluded from this note as they are out of any context.

Discussion

The number of these *in-situ* fossil bones found in the W. Maharashtra is quite small when compared with fossil finds in the central Narmada and in the Belan, a southernly tributary of the Ganges in Uttar Pradesh. But when we consider the general paucity of palaeontological material in the ancient alluvial deposits of the streams of the Peninsular India and especially of the W. Maharashtra—then these *in-situ* findings in the general context of geomorphological history of the region assume a great importance.

So far either in the Narmada or in the Godavari, the similar fossil species have been found in association with Early and Middle Stone Age tools, and hence the use of palaeontological material for dating cultural assemblages has become very limited. The fossil bones found at Paithan, spill-way fill of the Mula, Chandoli and at Bhivari are more or less associated with the Middle Stone Age tools. All these fossil species are definitely extinct and naturally the Middle Stone Age tools, from the gravel associations, are therefore not likely to be of Holocene period. In the light of the cultural development throughout the Old World the comparable industries like Middle Palaeolithic of Europe and Middle Stone

Age tools from Africa do not date to a period earlier than the early Upper Pleistocene or Last Interglacial. So naturally the Middle Stone Age tools in this context at least can not be earlier than Last Interglacial. However, if we accept the C-14 date from the Mula the whole filling is not likely to be older than 50 to 60 thousand years at the most, as the dated sample comes from almost the basal portion of the old alluvium. The Middle Stone Age tools in the Mula, the Pravara and the Godavari have been found in the more or less same geomorphological context and hence they can be dated to later part of the Upper Pleistocene.

There are very few Early Stone Age sites, occurring in stratified context in the W. Maharashtra. The sites of Gangapur on the Godavari and of Nevasa on the Pravara are perhaps the only best preserved evidences. At Gangapur the tool bearing horizon is slightly above the bed level of the Godavari while at Nevasa the boulder gravel of Hathi-Well is fast eroding and many times Middle Stone Age tools have been collected along with Early Stone Age tools from it. At Barod Garden, about 20 m. higher than the boulder gravel at Hathi-Well, again a mixed assemblage of Early and Middle Stone Age tools have been collected. It is only at Chirki, about 1½ km. down-stream of Nevasa, recently Corvinus has discovered and unearthed the camping cum workshop site of Early Stone Age man on the right bank of the Pravara. Here the level goes to a height of about 5-6 m. from the bed level of the Pravara and the Early Stone Age tools almost in mint condition and in all stages of manufacture have been found to occur in a thin rubble deposit resting on a rolling rocky surface. The Middle Stone Age tool-bearing alluvial gravel of varying thickness covers the rubble deposit. Thus the only well preserved sites of the Early Stone Age are at Gangapur and at Chirki-Nevasa. Technologically some of the tools are extremely well made and the use of the prepared core-technique is also not rare. The tools have been fashioned out of even bad raw materials. All these things suggest that the Early Stone Age man was technologically quite advanced. How old this advanced Early Stone Age industry of W. Maharashtra can be ?

It can not be earlier than the Middle Pleistocene if we consider the association of *Bos Namadicus* at Gangapur. But the *Bos Namadicus* occurs in association with the sample, dated to 33,000 B.P. in the Mula. Geomorphologically it has been found that the Godavari and its tributaries like the Pravara and the Mula were flowing at much lower level and more towards the south of the present course in the pre-depositional phase. The dating of this major erosional phase is not certain but can not be much earlier than Middle Pleistocene as the lowermost buried deposits have only preserved Middle Pleistocene fauna. Whatever may be the date of this early erosional phase, we can say, if only on the basis of faunal evidence, that the filling of these streams started in Middle Pleistocene. But in the light of the C-14 date the whole aggradational phase in the Godavari basin is likely to be of Upper Pleistocene only. In that case the Early Stone Age industry of Gangapur is more likely to date to Upper Pleistocene only. At Chirki, early man seems to have occupied the rocky plain at a time when the Pravara had just begun to fill its channel. If he would have been there earlier, the tools could have easily washed down into the valley because of the erosional phase of the streams. The cultural assemblage could get preserved in such a fine condition on a bare rolling rocky plain by the side of a river probably because it got sealed up by Middle Stone Age tool bearing channel without involving much time-gap between these two stages. All these points suggest that the occupation of the Chirki area was only in the earlier parts of the aggradational phase and there was not much time gap between the Early and Middle Stone Age traditions. If our dating of Middle

Stone Age tools to later part of the Upper Pleistocene is correct then it will not be very wrong if the Early Stone Age tools are placed in the early part of the Upper Pleistocene in the W. Maharashtra.

The dating of such advanced Early Stone Age industries to Upper Pleistocene in the Lower Narmada (Wainwright, 1964), in the Central Narmada at Mahadeo Piparia where Middle and Early Stone Age tools have been found together in the boulder conglomerate (Supekar, 1965), thus gets confirmed from the evidence obtained from W. Maharashtra. The Late Acheulian of sub-Saharan Africa (Clark, 1964), the Barda Balka Middle Palaeolithic of Iraq (Braidwood, 1960), and the Upper Stellenbosch—Late Sohan complex of West Pakistan (Paterson, 1962) have also been dated to the Upper Pleistocene and purely on comparative studies the chronology of Early Stone Age in W. Maharashtra dates more or less to the similar period.

Thus these fossil discoveries from W. Maharashtra have shown that :

(1) Some of the species which got extinct in Siwaliks in Early Pleistocene could survive almost till the end of the Upper Pleistocene, probably because of the better ecological setting, in the peninsula.

(2) The advanced Early Stone Age industries of Maharashtra are likely to be of Upper Pleistocene period.

(3) Geomorphologically the streams in Maharashtra have experienced considerable changes in their activities of cutting and filling in geologically speaking short time.

Acknowledgements

The author expresses his sincere thanks to Shri M. A. Chitale and Shri Oka of the Irrigation Deptt. Maharashtra state, for allowing to collect fossil bones from the Dam sites of the Mula and the Purana. He is extremely grateful to Shri Bholanath and Prof. T. S. Mahable of the Zoological Survey of India, Calcutta, and Botany Deptt., University of Poona for their palaeontological identifications and to the authorities of the Tata Institute of Fundamental Research, Bombay for C-14 dating of the sample from Mula Dam site.

NOTES

[1] R. J. Braidwood and B. Howe, *Prehistoric Investigations in Iraqui Kurdistan*, The University of Chicago, Illinois, 1960.

[2] J. D. Clark, ' The Prehistoric Origins of African Culture '. *Jr. of African History*, 2, No. 2, 1964, 162-183.

[3] R. V. Joshi, S. A. Sali and B. P. Bopardikar, ' Animal Fossil and Early Stone Age Tools from Gangapur on the Godavari River (Nasik dist., Maharashtra State) ', *Current Science*, No. 13, 1966, 344.

[4] A. P. Khatri, ' Origin and Development of Series II Culture of India ', *Proceedings of the Prehistoric Society for* 1962, XXVII, 1962, 191-208.

[5] T. T. Paterson and H. J. H. Drummond, *Soan the Palaeolithic of Pakistan*, Dept. of Archaeology, Govt. of Pakistan, Karachi, 1962.

[6] H. D. Sankalia, ' Middle Stone Age Culture in India and Pakistan, ' *Science*, 146, No. 3642, 1964, 365-375.

[7] S. G. Supekar, A Ph. D. thesis on the central Narmada, 1968.

[8] G. J. Wainwright, *The Pleistocene Deposits of the Lower Narmada River*, Baroda, 1964.

Plant Remains From Ancient Bhatkuli, District Amraoti, Maharashtra

by VISHNU-MITTRE and H. P. GUPTA

Introduction

The carbonised plant remains described in this paper have been discovered from Bhatkuli, district Amraoti, Maharashtra State, by Dr. Moreshwar G. Dikshit, the Director of Archives and Archaeology, Maharashtra, who very kindly sent the material to the senior author for investigation. As per personal communication from Dr. Dikshit, the material was discovered from a very preliminary investigation of the site and consequently nothing definite can be said about the age of the material and very likely it should be of early historic period.

The material is highly carbonised and is in the form of brittle blocks of ash and silt containing several food grains. The food grains except those of *Cicer arietinum* L. (chick-pea) are very fragile, but the morphological characters are well preserved. The food grains, recovered by breaking these blocks, are of two kinds, the chick-pea (*Cicer arietinum* L.) and spiklets of giant millet (*Sorghum* sp.). The latter are far more abundant than the former.

Description of Plant Remains

1. GIANT MILLET (JOWAR)
Sorghum sp.
(Plate II A ; Fig. 1)

The carbonised spikelets referred to Jowar are more or less lanceolate or oblong in shape. They measure 2.2 to 4.0 mm. in length and 2.0 to 3.0 mm. in breadth with the proximal side pointed and the distal side rounded. The hilum scar is prominently present on the flattened surface and the area bearing the embryo is prominently marked.

A comparison of the carbonised *Sorghum* seeds with that of modern Jowar seeds has revealed that the Bhatkuli specimens closely resemble in shape those of *Sorghum bicolor* as described by Bor (1960) [1]. The seeds are, however, much smaller and it may be due to shrinkage owing to charring. *Sorghum bicolor* is extensively cultivated in Bombay and Madras.

2. CHICK-PEA (GRAM OR CHANA)
Cicer Arietinum
(Plate II A; Fig. 2.)

Only twenty-four carbonised gram seeds have been recovered from the material. The seeds are obovate or subglobose in shape and prominently beaked, measuring 5.0—6.0 mm. in length, 3.5—4.0 mm. in breadth and 3.0—3.5 mm. in thickness. The hilum mark is well preserved. Some seeds are provided with wrinkles on the dorsal surface. The carbonised seeds are similar in shape but slightly smaller in size from those of modern chick-pea and this may be due to carbonization.

Discussion

Of the two plant remains discovered from the site the chick-pea (gram) is known for the first time from the archaeobotanical records in India. The remains of *sorghum* are known earlier from the chalcolithic site of Ahar (Vishnu-Mittre, 1968) [2]. The seeds of *Sorghum* from Ahar have been referred to *Sorghum vulgare*, whereas the Amraoti finds seem to belong to *Sorghum bicolor*. Thus *Sorghum* seems to have been known in India since the Chalcolithic period. Its cultural significance has already been commented upon by one of us (Vishnu-Mittre, *loc. cit*).

This discovery of chick-pea from Amraoti being the first record from India adds to our knowledge of the history of Indian cultivated plants. From this evidence alone it is, however, difficult to say that the chick-pea arrived in the country comparatively very late. From literary sources collected by Gode (1945) [3] it appears that it was chiefly used to feed horses from 800-1300 A.D., and chick-pea arrived in India together with the Persian and Arabic horses. Its use as food for horses in Kashmir is attested by *Rājtaranginī* but *Charaka Saṁhitā* mentions chick-pea as an article for food for human consumption amongst the Dhanyas.

Vavilov (1951)[4] believes that the western India is a part of the centre of origin for chick-pea. It seems that the chick-pea was domesticated in north-west India and later diffused into the other parts of the country. If the Persians or the Arabians should be held responsible for its introduction and diffusion into the country then their possible routes might have been either through the north-west India or through the Thana Coast in Bombay which had an important port for exchanges between West Indians, Egyptians, Phoenicians, Babylons, Greeks, Persians and the Arabic people. It is hoped that the continued researches in Archaeobotany in India will eventually establish if chick-pea has really been a late arrival in the country or has been known in India since the ancient times.

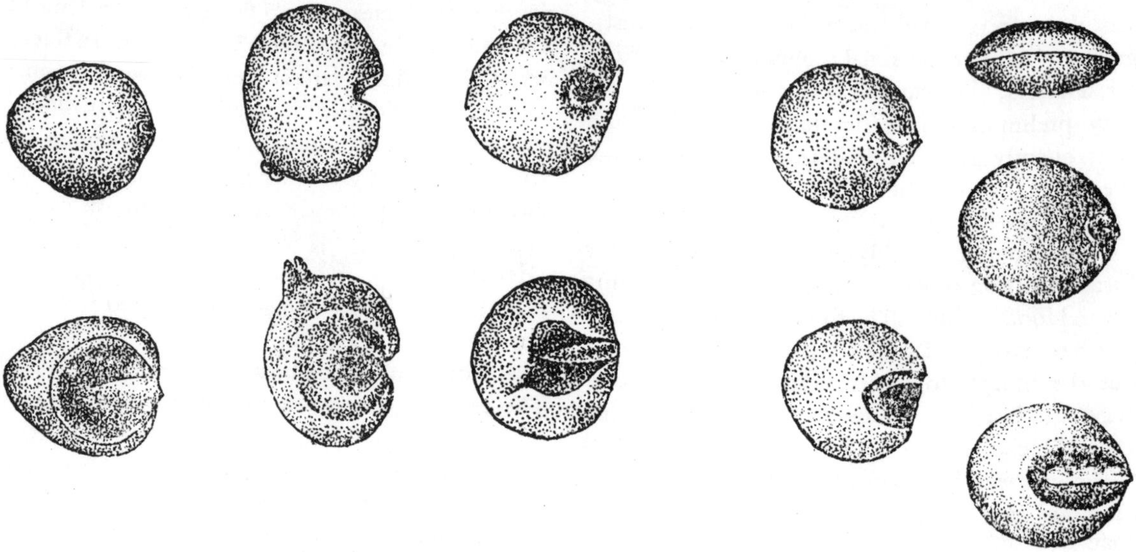

Fig. 1. Carbonised seeds of *Sorghum* sp. shown in different views X 7.

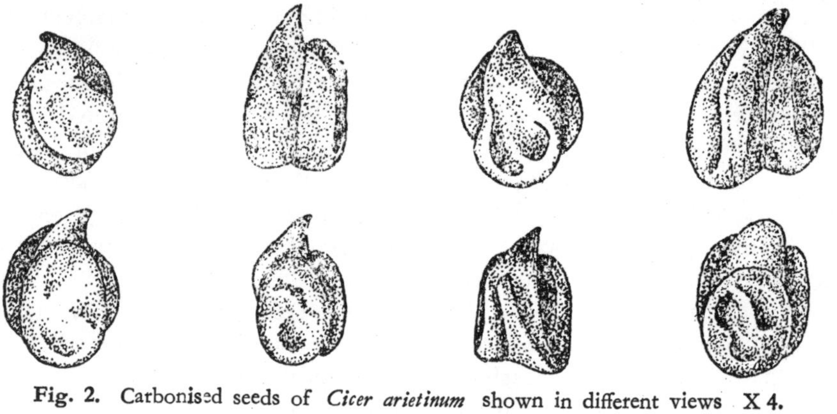

Fig. 2. Carbonised seeds of *Cicer arietinum* shown in different views X 4.

NOTES

[1] N. L. Bor, *The Grasses of Burma, Ceylon, India and Pakistan*. I, Oxford, London, New York, Paris, 1959.

[2] Vishnu-Mittre, 'Plant Economy in Ancient Ahar, Rajasthan.' in '*The City of Tambavati*' by H. D. Sankalia, Poona, 1968.

[3] P. K. Gode, 'Studies in the hisory of Indian plants—History of Canaka (gram) as food for horses between A.D. 800 and 1870 together with some notes on the import of foreign horses into ancient India in Medieval times', *Ann. Bor. Inst*. 26 (1—2), 1945, 89-105.

[4] N. I. Vavilov, *The Origin, Variation, Immunity and Breeding of Cultivated Plant*, New York, 1951.

Determining the Techniques of Handmade and Wheel-Turned Pottery by Microscopic Analysis

by S. P. GUPTA

In the beginning earthen pots were made by hand alone ; wheel-made pottery appeared quite late, probably, between 3,000 and 2,500 B.C. The transition from the hand-made pottery to the wheel-turned pottery was gradual. At an early stage the wheel used for making pottery was a slow-moving one, with the result, the surface of the wheel-turned pots did not often reveal, to the naked eye, the characteristic feature of a pot made on a fast moving wheel, i.e. clear-cut striation marks of the fingers which, sometimes create an effect of concentric channeling or fluting all along the body of the pot. Henry Frankfort has further pointed out that the " ..wheel-made pottery may not show clear traces of 'wheel-marks', since pots were frequently wheel finished for about two-thirds of their height and then roughly cut away from the mass of the clay on the wheel "[1]. It has been, therefore, difficult to determine precisely the period during which the wheel-made pottery was introduced. Archaeological literature is full of such statements which show this difficulty in clear-cut terms. A. Lucas, in his famous book entitled '*Ancient Egyptian Materials and Industries*' gives a vivid description of this state of affairs. He writes that " the date of the introduction of the wheel is a matter of some controversy." Miss D. Billington suggests that the necks of some pre-Dynastic pots may have been turned on a slow wheel, and Petrie states that " the first use of the wheel regularly is for the great jars of the royal factory in the I Dynasty". Reisner, however, says that the beginning of wheel-made pottery dates from the period between the reign of Khasekhemui and the accession of Snofru, and Frankfort states that the potter's wheel was only generally used in Egypt " about the Fourth Dynasty, though sporadically appearing since the First ". Junker maintains that "all prehistoric and Early Dynastic pottery was made by hand, and that the wheel was only introduced during the Old Kingdom "[2].

Clearly enough, an urgent need is felt to observe pottery produced by different methods, more closely and scientifically than hitherto. A state has come when we cannot just give our opinion haphazardly. We must be able to substantiate the truth of our statements from every possible angle, only keeping in view that our criterion should be, as far as possible, more objective than subjective.

Last year I took up a village of Delhi, called 'Chirag Dilli', situated on a connecting road between Hauz Khas and Kalkaji for my sociological studies of the potters and potteries and presented a paper 'Sociology of Pottery : Chirag Dilli a case study,' to the Seminar on Pottery organized by the University of Patna. Some of the participants later on suggested to me to study the technological aspect of the pottery produced in the village also. I could do a little in this field now and the results of my preliminary work are presented here. They are, in fact, tentative since they are based on a few samples only. More data is being collected and a fuller report will follow in due course of time. I do not know how far this communication will help the archaeoloical laboratories to conduct some similar tests on the ancient potteries, but it is hoped that the observations placed below might lead to better objective methods to solve a difficult problem before the archaeologists.

The apparatus used in the present case is only a microscope. So far I have used one with only 60 times magnification, although in the case of pots of very well levigated clay one with more magnification (say upto 200, or even 300 times) may be required. I also propose to use stereo-microscope coupled with stereo-photographic camera for three dimentional photographs. It may be absolutely necessary in the case of pots made on slow-wheels.

The clay used by the potters at Chirag Dilli is normally not very fine. It contains heavier and coarser grains of silica and other minerals. Often, it is mixed with different tempering materials like husk particles sometimes containing grains, animal dung with small particles of grass, hair of animals, even particles of pottery collected after crushing the old pots with stones.

When a lump of this clay is thrown of a potter's wheel all the mineral particles, husk and grain pieces, etc. are in the form of a levigated mixed mass. The moment the wheel is moved and the clay lump begins to change into some shape due to the combined action of the rotating wheel and the pressure of fingers, the particles and pieces within the clay can no longer remain in the same position. In fact, the very process of enlargement of a small lump of clay into a big pot implies a complete rearrangement of these particles in the body-fabric.

Now the simple question is whether by observing the arrangement of these particles in general and heavier and bigger particles of different materials in particular, and also of the husk-pieces can we make out the forces and the process which created this phenomenon ? Probably, we can. The physical changes, unless completely obliterated by later disturbances of total burnishing and the like, are susceptible to identification.

It has been observed on the unbaked pots that the coarser and heavier particles of the clay used are arranged one behind the other along the ridge created in between the two concentric channels produced by the fingers. Their direction of arrangement followed the direction of the rotation of the wheel. Similar was the case with the husk and grain pieces also. The post-fired pots showed the same arrangement of the particles and burnt husk and grain pieces. If some of these pieces were completely burnt up; the resultant voids or holes are clearly found placed along the same ridges.

This happens because of the centrifugal action. Take some sand in a test tube and pour in some water. Rotate the tube in a centrifuge and the heavier particles are thrown out and separated. Although, the plasticity of the clay considerably retards this centrifugal action and acts against the force working for the centrifugal process, the coarser and heavier particles still manage to jump over the controlling force of the plasticity of the clay. Since between the two fingers moving along, the walls of pot create a space where a ridge is automatically formed between the two channels or flutings created by the fingers, the coarser and heavier grains thrown away from the centre find another hurdle in the ridge and get stuck up. In the case of lighter husk pieces the concentric arrangement may not occur in all the cases although due to the force of the fingers they too get a directional change in their placement which too roughly follow the path of the fingers.

Closely connected with it is another observation in the case of wheel-made pottery. Take a large number of measurements of the thickness of a pot both on the horizontal and vertical planes. A definite regularity is found along the channels with alternating ridges : we can determine the ridge, if along one horizontal plane the thickness is more than in the other. Thus we have alternating series of thickness—one of lower denominations and the other higher. This indicates respectively the channeling and ridging, and, therefore, the use of wheel.

A third observation is made along the vertical section of the walls of the pot. Since the basic feature of a wheel-turned pot is the formation of channels and ridges, the sections of the pots under proper magnification and observation under stereomicroscope do show zig zag profile along the edges. The zig zag formation is regular inconsonance with the formation of the channel and ridge.

However, there is a serious pit-fall in this analysis against which a worker should guard himself. H. Frankfort had said that ' Deductions based on the appearance of early pottery are apt to be misleading, for pots built up by hand on a table turned on the ground may well have traces of ' wheel-marks' ". By this he meant the irregular striation marks of the fingers. To some extent it is true but pots made by the turn-table, also known as ' Turnette ' method will normally not have regular formation of channels and ridges. By its very nature, the method of turn-table' can rarely produce regular fluting. In this process a small wooden plank or basket, on which the pot to be-made is kept, is turned again and again by the potter himself or one of his assistants sitting nearby. This turning of the plank or the table, unless mechanically operated on a pivot, cannot be regulated for the spinning movement of the wheel and, therefore, at definite intervals both the channels and the ridges would show breaks in the form of kinks which must be clearly looked for and marked. It is a sign which definitely militates against the use of a true wheel.

Now, I come to the hand-made pottery. Needless to say that the absence of regular channels and ridges is clearly seen in this category of pots. When I observed a potter making a hand-made pot, I found that he is using the palms of his hands. A stationary pot, unless there is a sure and flat base, which is not the case with a pot in-making, cannot be held in position with the help of fingers alone. It is only when a pot is rotating, it can be shaped and held in position over the wheel with a feathery light touch of the fingers just as fast moving cycles can be balanced without holding the handles even. Thus when the palms are used we do not get regular flutings, instead broad patches are seen. The particles are also not arranged in any regular fashion. The thickness of the walls of pots also behaves erratically. The overall shape of the pot is also not well-formed. In the case of 4,000 year old hand-made pot from Shahi Tump in Baluchistan an attempt was made to reduce the erratic thickness of the walls of the pots to some uniformity by scrapping off the extra clay at several places by a comb like scraper.

I also tried to observe the pots which were used as water-pitchers. At the first instance a small pot with extra-thick walls was made on the wheel. It was then allowed to dry a little. When it is in the leather hard condition, a wooden dabbar and a terrocotta support were used to enlarge the body by all round beating the small pot and reducing the thickness of the walls. Pots made by this technique have sometimes shown the particles, etc. dispersed radially—perhaps due to beating of the clay. However, this observation in one or two cases need further evidence.

The results presented here, I must repeat it, are absolutely tentative based on very few pots I got made, though under my close observations. More pots will be made and more observations recorded in coming months. Once these are perfected I propose to apply them on the prehistoric pottery to work out the history of wheel-turned pots of India and the world as well.

NOTES

[1] H. Frankfort, *Studies in Early Pottery of the Near East*, I,8. London, 1962, 369.

[2] A. Lucas, *Ancient Egyptian Materials and Industries*

[3] Ibid.

New Light on Central Indian Archaeology Through Kayatha Excavations

by V. S. WAKANKAR

The main work of the excavation was taken over at Kayatha, a small town 15 miles east of Ujjain on the Ujjain-Maksi Road. This site is known to have been the native place of Varahamihir and dedicated to Chitragupta (Yama's secretary), as it is said that he made penances at Kayatha and particularly at a place called Gad Maruti where we dug one of our trenches. During the two excavation seasons (1965 and, '66) four trenches were undertaken, two at Gad Maruti and two on the eastern of Toda Mound. As a result of the excavations of these four trenches we reached the following conclusions which will give us a brief story of culture sequence of the site.

The first settlement at this site started when it was densely forested. Occassionally people using microlithic tools did pass through the site but never settled. The people, whose cultural epicentre seems to be at some other place, came down to settle in this rich black cotton soil area, rich in food and water. They used to build mud houses, covered them either with grass or mud roofing called *'Ora'*.

The *Ora* is a mud roofed house with wooden supports. The mud has been plastered on the roof on either bamboos or cotton and millet branches. The authors of this culture used sturdy vessels manufactured by high speed wheel technique. The surface was slipped by dark brown cream, mauve, purple, black and yellow-ochre slips, burnished finely to give the surface a fine lustre. The surface was then decorated by multi-coloured designs and parallel bands. The technique generally gives an impression of the Harappan style and may prove to be contemporary of late Harappan industry. The shapes also show affinity with some Harappan and some pre-Harappan elements, found in Rajasthan and Punjab. This phase, which we may call as Kayatha Phase I culture, gives a rather interesting pottery sequence. The painted Black-and-Red ware, which is aboundantly found in Ahar and other chalcolithic sites of Malwa-Rajasthan complex and which is associated with the Harappan element in Gujarat and Saurashtra, is totally missing here in this phase and it may be because of the preoccurrence of this cultural tradition.

During this period which is dated to 1965±-100 B.C., the site was hit by two local floods of the river Choti Kalishindh which is just flowing by the mounds. Kalishindh (Choti Kalishindh) is a tributary of the Chambal and is also referred as Gargara in one of the inscriptions of the Western Guptas found at Gangadhar which is also a chalcolithic site on the same river.

This earliest culture of Malwa, which we are tempted to call as 'Kayatha Culture' was followed by another culture marked by its profusely found white painted black-and-red pottery. The pottery of this type was associated with Harappa Culture in Gujarat and Saurashtra but also had its independant growth at Ahar (a site near Udaipur town of Rajasthan), Manoti and Awra. At Manoti a site which has now been submerged under the Chambal waters, this type of pottery was found in its earliest phases (i.e.pre-citadel and citadel phase) and is associated with Harappan remains represented by typical Harappan jar, soapstone decorated seal and mud brick wall resting over a platform.

Phase II. : In Kayatha this cultural phase is mostly represented by black-and-red ware, painted mostly on the outer surface of carinated bowls and Burnished Red ware with light and out-flaring rim. The earlier rough pottery still continues in abundance showing either a cultural migrations or a gradual evolution.

The earliest phase of nomadic hunters is marked by the use of microlithic tools and mesolithic implements but Phases I and II are marked by the use of copper (a copper bar and a few copper objects including a copper bracelet were found along with other remains). The most important finds from these cultural deposits (PhaseII) are the terracottas which were found in abundance and much stylised figures of bulls with prominent hump and horns but no legs, no ears and no head. Some of them are decorated by serpantine lines and cresecnt marks. So far such fiigures are unknown from any chalcolithic site in India but bulls with crescent decorations have been found at Harappan sites.

Malwa chalcolithic, better known as Nagda-Maheshwar culture, follows this earlier culture. Remains of this culture have been unearthed at Navdatoli, Maheshwar, Nagda, Eran, Awra, Pasewa and Monoti . This is represented by profusely decorated Malwa red ware and is also associated by a type of coarse grey ware which is quite different from the northern Painted Grey Ware. Painted black on red or black on cream, is mostly marked by its dishes and cups having stands.

Portions of two burnt houses were exposed in KTH—1 and KTH—4 Trenches dating to some three and a half millennia before our era. The western part of the locality was suddenly destroyed by fire. The houses being made of bamboo and mud plaster nothing intact survived. The floors of the houses were generally paved with burnt lumps of clay and hydrolic lime. Stone balls, querns, and pestles, many earthen pots, dishes and cups-on-stand, beautifully decorated *Choclas*, and posthole marks on the floors were detected.

The site does not show any remarkable gap between different cultural deposits of historic and prehistoric eras. Iron-using people followed the earlier people. Copper ear ornaments, ivory figures of mother goddess, agate and jasper beads, iron tools, terracotta figures and *tatanka chakras* have been found from these deposits. Northern Black Polished ware pieces along with Painted Grey ware also were found with these antiquities. Then follows the Sunga period denoted by broken terracottas. Kushan glazed ware and terracotta figures have also been found. Cast copper coins bearing *Swastika* on one side and on another side the *Shadarchakra*, human-figure and *Swastika* were found on the floor of a house of this period. Conch shell bangles were also found in all historic deposits.

During the Gupta period, deposits of a house with a kitchen-room, where a *Choola*, a basin, pestle and quern were unearthed, a terrocotta figure of lord Buddha in standing pose was found lying on the floor in that kitchen.

A house of the early Parmar period was exposed in the upper layers of Trench 1. This had a small room and a hall paved with small bricks measuring 8"×12"×2". The house had brick walls mortared in sticky grey soil. The western wall was completely destroyed by brick robbers. No antiquity worth dating was found on the surface of the house. But it has been noticed throughout the site that wherever Parmar images were lying, brick pavements, plinths and walls have been observed. The covering layers at the top yielded few coins of Shah Mohammad Shah, and probably he is responsible for the destruction of all lofty temples of this site.

Thus the site with a maximum deposit of 40 feet has revealed all the major phases of the

Malwa culture through different ages and throw new light on the oldest cultural remains of this region.

This site is extensive and now is divided in several mounds known with different names, Toda and Gad being the oldest, while Bada Bazar developed during the Maratha period under Holkars of Indore. A new locality known as Adarsha Nagar is now developing south of this town. During our explorations images of Shesha Shayi Vishṇu, Surya, Shiva, Parvati, Keechak, Ganesh, Kamdhenu and head of Vishnu were found.

Parmar images and architectural pieces are lying all over the site and indicate towards a terrible destruction during the Muslim invasions. The town regains its glory during Rajput Maratha supremacy and huge buildings and temples were erected to enrich the site. The Jain temple is having a rich collection of manuscripts. A place of Holkar Dynasty still stands in the central part of the town and contains paintings in the Rajput style.

This site is rich in antiquities and the excavation has yielded more than 1,000 antiquities. The University proposes to continue the work to have more data to know about the material achievement of the oldest habitations in Kayatha.

Kayatha has proved to be the southernmost site where Painted Grey ware, painted Malwa ware, painted black-and-red ware as well as late Harappan ware which was named by us as 'Kayatha ware' because of its discovery in this site in a well stratified position, were recovered during the excavation.

The extent of Harappan influence in the heart of Malwa plateau is in itself of great importance, and many questions arise because of the new discovery. Who were the people who adopted this culture, still remains a problem as no skeletal evidence had been found at Kayatha. Either these were the local people who gradually developed a rural culture or belonged to a wave of people from outside who migrated to this part of the country which had heavily humid climate and vast stretch of furtile and rich agricultural plain.

Due to some catastorphe, about which there is little known information, which occured in Sindh and Rajasthan, the furtile alluvial valleys of Sindhu (Indus) and Saraswati became quite dry (at the beginning of third millennium B.C.) and the people started moving east to find suitable habitable land. The affinity of the pottery shapes and fabric of Kayatha ware with Harappan ware, as well as a few incised signs on potsherds with the Harappan script definitely prove that there were traditional contacts. The absence of burnt brick houses is due to the economic depression which must have taken place due to the exodus. These people brought with them the art of bronze casting as is evident from the finds at Kayatha, these consist of a bronze bar, bronze bracelet and copper wire. The Harappan complicated design on pottery is absent and it has been replaced by simple designs which apparently give pre-Harappan appearance. It is the real source of later Malwa painted ware.

When the Black-and-red ware culture overcame this earlier culture, the pottery tradition had a sudden break. The earlier ceramic industry and the developed metallurgy and many other traditions disappear with the arrival of this new but definitely inferior culture. Only the rough utilitarian pottery continued.

The new Malwa ceramic industry generally known as painted Black on red or Malwa—Jorwe, ware, which developed with its multipurpose designing and shapes indicates a flourishing cultural tradition. Who were responsible for introducing this cultural elements ? A few scholars tried to link this new ceramic industry with those of Gian and Susa and other sites of Mesopotamia but the time span between the two is over a thousands year and so this affinity may simply be supperficial. The real source of dishes-on-stands, big *Lotas* and spouted bowls is definitely earlier and germinated in Kayatha industry.

Who were the people responsible for the growth of the Indian chalcolithic cultures is yet to be decided. Vedic people, who developed their cultural traditions in the river valleys of Sindhu (Indus), Saraswati and western part of Ganga plains might be the authors of these cultures. Malwa as the Puranic history goes, was occupied by the Awantas in Vedic days. The Haihayas followed them and had an extensive empire, but they were terribly routed by the Bhargavas of Bhṛigukachchha of Gujarat. They were again driven back by the Haihayas to gain a long peaceful reign. Whether these Puranic legends had to do something with these different cultural waves is yet to be decided, we will have to wait few more years till the decipherment of the Harappan script and that only will finalise the issue.

Malwa Chalcolithic cultures were followed by Pradyotas of Ujjaini who developed a very poor type of ceramic industry probably because they had developed metal industry and made their finer requirements of copper and iron. But they brought Painted Grey ware and Northern Black Polished ware from the Ganga Valley. Kayatha that way, is also very important as it has yielded several pieces of Painted Grey ware, this being the southernmost site so far yielding that ware.

What was going on in this area when the Harappa culture was at its zenith is partially revealed through the new excavation at Kayatha. The university proposes to continue the work and get still more information about this earlist culture of Malwa.

Radio-Carbon dates for Kayatha Chalcolithic cultures are as follows;—

Painted Grey ware	2,420±100 B.P.
Malwa chalcolithic culture	3,690±100 B.P.
Painted Black & Red ware	3,915±110 B.P.
Kayatha ware	3,665±100 B.P.

Rajghat Copper—A Metallurgical View

by H.C. BHARDWAJ

Archaeological excavations at Rajghat (Distt. Varanasi) conducted by Banaras Hindu University have brought to light a continuous cultural sequence from about 800 B.C. to modern times. A large number of copper and bronze objects have been recovered during the excavations. A few of them, all from period I (circa 800 B. C. to 200 BC) have been chemically analysed and a few examined metallographically.

Experimental Procedure

Scheme of Chemical Analysis : In order to obtain analysis the samples were made free from the corrosion products. The metallic surface was further cleaned by means of a clean file.

The sample was dissloved in nitric acid and the solution was diluted and digested. The residue if any (the residue consists of hydrated tin oxide & silica) was filtered off. To know the net weight of SnO_2, the residue was ignited with NH_4I to volatilize SnO_2 by Caley's method. [1]. The residue was further treated with nitric acid to recover any metallic constituent and the residue left was weighed and reported as insoluble residue. Mostly it consists of silica.

The filtrate from tin separation was treated with HCl to test the presence of silver which however was found to be absent, as there was no turbidity or ppt. To the above solution itself conc. H_2SO_4 was added and the solution treated till copious white fumes were liberated and then digested with water and any precipitate of $PbSO_4$ filtered.

The above filtrate was treated and a current of H_2S was passed. The precipitate was collected over filter paper. The filtrate was treated with yellow ammonium sulphide and filtrate tested for arsenic and antimony.

The residue was dissolved in HNO_3, evaporated with H_2SO_4 to white fumes, and copper precipitated as cuprous thiocyanate.

Filtrate from H_2S precipitate was treated with nitric acid and iron precipitated with NH_4OH. Nickel was determined in the filtrate as dimethylglyoxime complex. Cobalt was tested in the filtrate with α Nitroso β naphthol.

Determination of Arsenic and Antimony

Quantitative estimation of arsenic was made in case of Specimen No. 6, on a separate sample. The sample was dissolved in conc. HNO_3 and after removal of excess of nitric acid the nitrates were decomposed and the residual material was dissolved in conc. HCl. Requisite amount of ferrous sulphate was added to ensure their continuation in reduced form and the solution was distilled at 108°C. A current of H_2S was passed into the distillate and the precipitate filtered through sintered glass crucible, washed with a mixture of CS_2 and alcohol, dried and weighed and percentage of arsenic calculated from the weight of As_2S_3.

Further distillation was carried out at a higher temperature upto 200°C and H_2S passed, but the amount of antimony was too small for quantitative estimation.

Determination of Sulphur. Determination of sulphur was done on separate samples. The sample was decomposed with HNO_3 and any residue filtered. The filtrate was treated with HCl, and evaporated to remove excess of nitric acid, the residue was again treated with dil HC1 and

S (present as sulphate) was precipitated with $BaCl_2$ in hot solution and weighed as $BaSO_4$.

Metallographic Examination : The specimens were mounted in bakelite at a maximum temperature of 150°C and maximum load of half a ton. They were ground over successively finer grades of emery papers (from one zero to four zero) and then polished on silvet cloth on rotating discs containing fine alumina abrasive powder, finally these were given a finishing hand polish with brasso. The as polished surfaces were examined under metallurgical microscope to reveal non-metallic inclusions. Then the surfaces were etched, with ferric chloride solutions ($FeCl_3$ 10 gms., conc. HC1 30 c.c., water 120 c.c.) or (Ammonium hydroxide—conc. 10 c.c., H_2O_2—1.00 c.c.) etching removes the thin deformed layer produced by polishing and provides contrast to the various microstructural constituents.

Results of Chemical analysis (See table below)

From the table below, we find that sample No. 1 and 2 are of bronze and 3rd contains 1.6% of tin, samples 4, 5 and 6 are of unalloyed copper. In unalloyed copper samples the maximum percentage of copper is 98.05 and minimum copper content is 95.45%. The balance of 2 to 4.5% is distributed amongst impurities. Major impurities are lead, iron, nickel, calcium oxide, magnesium oxide, sulphur and oxygen (O_2 has not been chemically determined but its qualitative presence was marked during metallographic examination. O_2 has in all the cases been determined only by difference).

Significance of Impurities

Sulphur : Sulphur is present in all the specimens from traces to O.75%, this might suggest the use of sulphide ores (as copper has great affinity for sulphur there could also be some chances of sulphur entering through other sources) [2]. The quantity of sulphur in the final product would depend upon degree of roasting. Lesser the sulphur greater has been the roasting. It might be of interest to mention that cuprous sulphide undergoes no change without excess of air, when excess of air is available sulphur is partially converted to SO_2 which escapes out, partly it is converted into sulphuric acid which forms copper sulphate, which decomposes only if temperature is raised to strong red heat. Normally some sulphur would always be left in copper. For complete removal of sulphur the metal should be thoroughly molten, when SO_2 will escape out, any shaking and poling further helps the escape of SO_2. In earlier periods the metal was not always kept in molten condition for long time, and so some SO_2 always remained entraped. [3]

Iron : Iron is present in all specimens and its content varies from 0.21% to 2.23%. Its source could be the sulphide ore, which have iron pyrites associated with it. Most of the iron is quite easily removed from copper during smelting, as there are very little chances of iron oxide being, reduced to metallic state, most of it passes into slags, its variable content could be on account of slight changes in the smelting conditions. Its presence along with that of sulphur suggests the use of sulphide ores. Its presence might also indicate the lack of thorough and prolonged melting.

Nickel, Cobalt, Arsenic, Antimony

The sulphide ores of copper are always associated with a number of metallic elements e.g. Fe, Co, Ni, Mo, Ag, Au, As, Sb, Sn, Pb, Cd, Zn, Se and Te etc. Some of these or all of these might be present in a particular ore. Few of these elments might be removed completely or partially during smelting due to their volatilization e.g. As, Sb, Cd, Zn, while a few others baser than copper e.g. Sn, Co, Ni, Fe, Pb, could be at least partially removed by oxidation and slagging, while nobler metals like Ag or Au are enriched during smelting.

TABLE SHOWING THE RESULT OF CHEMICAL ANALYSIS OF RAJGHAT COPPER OBJECTS

Sr. No.	Nature of the object	Period	Appr. Date	Ins. or Residue	Cu %	Sn %	Pb %	As %	Sb %	Fe %	Ni %	Co %	CaO %	MgO %	S %	O2 by diff. %	Total
1.	Coin (Bronze)	1 C	300 BC 200 BC	—	86.90	7.83	0.83	+	N.D.	1.50	1.07	+	N.D.	N.D.	Tr.	1.87	100.00
2.	Bronze fragment	1 C	400 BC 200 BC	0.84	79.40	13.99	0.09	Tr.	Tr.	2.23	N.D.	+	2.46	0.74	Tr.	—	99.75
3.	Piece of a copper Bangle	1 C	400 BC 200 BC	0.32	93.93	1.82	Tr.	+	N.D.	1.09	0.32	N.D.	1.86	0.38	0.48		100.20
4.	Copper Fragment	1 B	600 BC 400 BC	—	98.05	—	Tr.	+	+	0.37	0.08	N.D.	0.85	0.17	Tr.	—	99.52
5.	Antimony Rod	1 B	600 BC 400 BC	—	96.38	—	—	+	—	0.21	0.08	N.D.	2.31	0.84	0.75	—	100.57
6.	Piece of a copper sheet	1 B	600 BC 400 BC	—	95.45	—	—	0.25	Tr.	0.96	0.15	+	1.75	N.D.	0.20	1.24	100.00

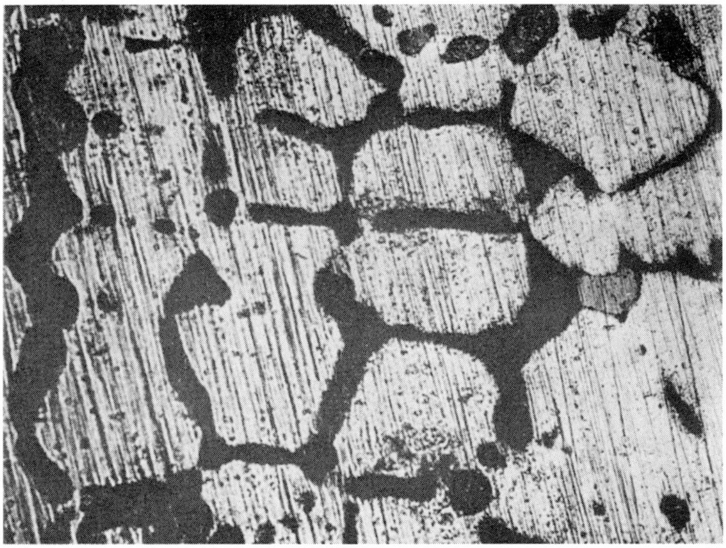

A. Photomicrographs showing micro-constituents of specimen No. 1 x 200 (unetched), showing low melting inclusions as grain boundary network dislodged during grinding.

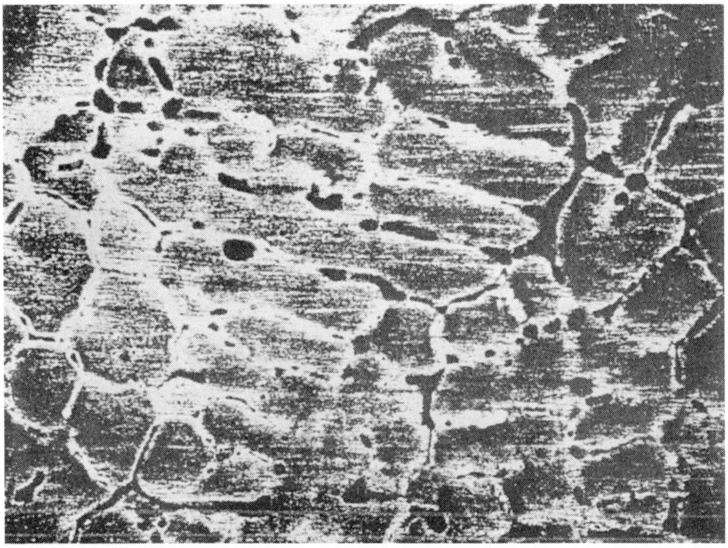

B. Photomicrograph showing micro-constituents of specimen No. 1 x 100 Etched with NH_4OH+ H_2O_2 showing cast structure with coring. Lighter etching bands are copper rich, interior tin rich.

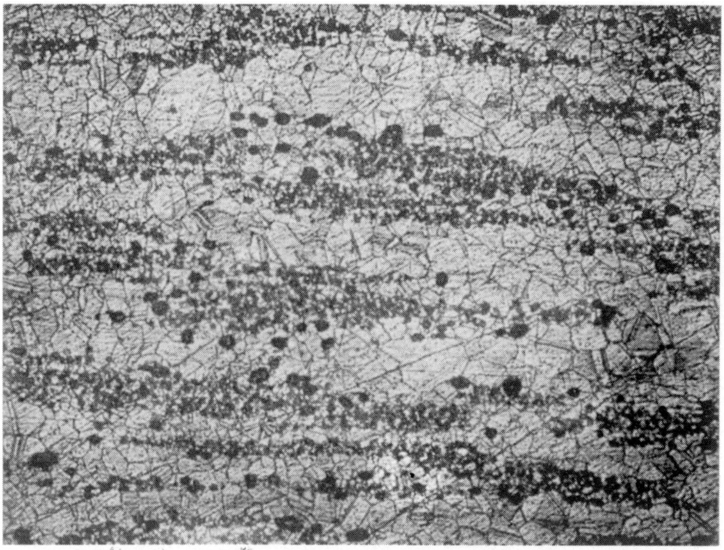

A. Photomicrograph showing micro-constituents of specimen No. 6 x 200. Etched with $NH_4OH+H_2O_2$ showing hot worked globular eutectic, alternate banding, recrystalized finer grains and finer eutectic.

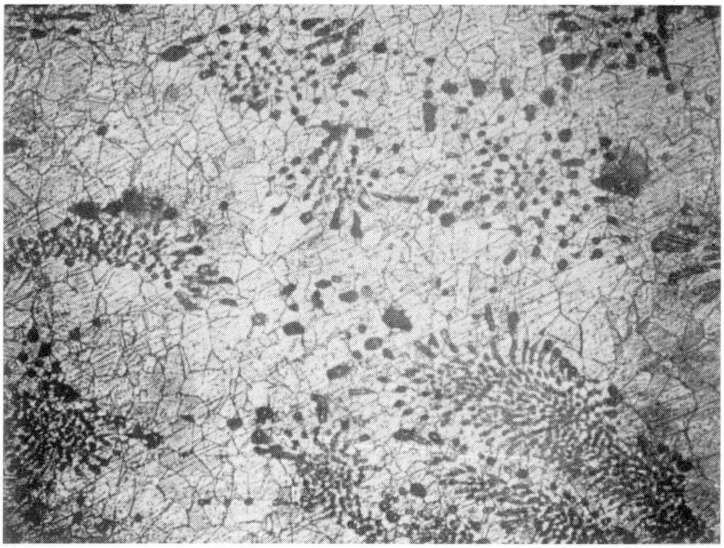

B. Photomicrograph showing micro-constituents of specimen No. 6 x 200 Etched with Fe Cl solution. (Flat surface) Eutectic percentage about 8%.

Nickel : Nickel has strong affinity for copper and on that account whenever the ore has nickel content some of it would be invariably found in the metal extracted. Though normally nickel should go into slag, yet it is always retained in the metal to some extent. When ore has a high content of nickel, the first few percentages of nickel pass into slag, but when amount of nickel decreases slagging becomes slower and the removal of the last portion is most difficult. Further nickel oxide is soluble in copper and hence its chances of retention in the melt are always there. If the reducing conditions prevail in the furnace, nickel oxide is reduced to metal and is absorbed by copper [4]

Cobalt : Cobalt behaves like iron during extraction of the metal. It is readily oxidized and slagged off. However if ore contains higher percentage of cobalt, it would require considerable time for its removal, its smaller content as compared to iron is on account of its comparative low percentage in the ore itself.

Lead : Lead is present in most of these specimens in small quantity and its source must be the impurity in the ore itself, lead when present in the ore is supposed to be persistent impurity. However, if slag is acid, its removal is favoured.

Tin : Except the 1st three specimens (in which tin seems to be deliberate addition) it is otherwise absent. So there is no proof of the ore containing tin. However tin when present in small quantities will be eliminated if the slag is basic.

Arsenic and Antimony : These elements partly volatilize during smelting but are not eliminated completely. Bray [5] mentions that distribution ratio of arsenic in slag to arsenic in the metal is over 500 to 1. During roasting As and Sb volatilize as As_2O_3 and Sb_2O_3, but some of these are converted to As_2O_5 and Sb_2O_5 which are less volatile, which form non-volatile arsenate and antimonate with copper. Amount of As and Sb would depend upon the nature of the atmosphere during roasting [6].

CaO, MgO : The presence of CaO and MgO suggests the presence of slag particles and may even indicate insufficient melting. The intake of CaO and MgO can also be due to the melt attacking the refractory material of the furnace.

Metallographic Examination

Specimen No. 1. (Pl. III A) : When examined metallographically in an unetched section reveals low melting inclusions as grain boundary net work, which have been dislodged during grinding. The examination of the etched section (Pl. III B) reveals cast structure, coring is clearly visible due to the segregation of tin on solidification. This coring effect might be attributed to comparatively fast rate of solidification. (It is clear that unless time is allowed for adjustment of varying crystal concentrations during freezing, the crystal has an inhomogenous structure, resulting in dendritic segregation or coring.) In the Pl. III B the lighter etching bands are copper rich, interior is the tin rich. The specimen has a hardness of V.H. N. 66. This is a low hardness for a bronze sample and can be attributed to the low melting grain boundary inclusions.

*Specimen No.*6 Metallographic examination of Sp.No.6 (Pl. IVA & B), shows hot worked metal, copper—copper oxide eutectic is also visible as globular alternate banding(Pl. IV A). The grains are finer in size and look to be recrystallized. Annealing twins are visible throughout the section as evidence of heat treatment above the recrystallization temperature. The examination of flat surface shows (Pl. IV B) that the eutectic is about 8 to 10%.

The hardness at V.H.N. is 112. This increased hardness is due to finer grain size and finer eutectic..

The author is thankful to Prof. A.K. Narain, Head of the Department of Ancient Indian History, Culture and Archaeology of Banaras Hindu University, for providing facilities and giving encouragement throughout this work. Thanks are also due to Prof. T.R. Anantharaman, Head of the Department of Metallurgy, and Dr. S. Misra of the Metallurgy Department, B.H.U. for providing facilities for the metallographic examination.

NOTES

[1] E. R. Caley & H. G. Burford, *Ind. Eng. Chem. Anal* Ed. 8, 114, 1936.

[2] R. F. Tylecote, *Metallurgy in Archaeology*, 27.

[3] W. Gowland, *Nonferrous metals*, 54.

[4] D. M. Liddle, *Hand Book of Non-Ferrous Metallurgy*, 1945, 245.

[5] J. L. Bray, *Non-Ferrous Metallurgy*, 1947, 200.

[6] Joseph Newton and Curtis L. Wilson, *Metallurgy of Copper*, 1942, 70.

Chalcolithic Burials : The Tekwada Evidence

by M. K. DHAVALIKAR

Consequent upon the discovery of the post-Harappan chalcolithic phase in Indian Proto-history, a considerable number of sites have so far been excavated in Central India, 'Western India and the Deccan. Of these, the chalcolithic cultures of the Deccan are characterised by burials which, on account of their variety, are indeed worthy of special attention. Besides providing us clues to the racial characteristics of the authors of the chalcolithic settlers they have also yielded valuable information concerning the eschatological beliefs of these pioneering colonizers. The burials themselves, as is usually the case, are rich in their contents which comprise a variety of vessels which once contained food and water for the deceased, his ornaments and his tools and weapons, mostly lithic. There is ample evidence, stratigraphical and otherwise, to show that the burials belong to the authors of the Nasik-Jorwe culture which has now firmly been assigned, on the basis of the C-14 determinations, to the time bracket *circa* 1,500 B.C. to 1,000 B.C.

The chalcolithic burials of Maharashtra were first encountered at Tekwada (District Jalgaon, which is situated on the left bank of river, Girna, a truibutary of Tapti. As the Cemetery lies just across the Viven opposite the habitation site at Bahal, it seems most likely that it belongs to the earliest settlers of Bahal. Later still, chalcolithic burials were also discovered at Nevasa, Chandoli, Daimabad and several other sites in the Deccan. They can be classified into three distinct categories namely, (i) the pit burial with extended skeleton, (ii) the single urn burial and (iii) twin or multiple urn burial. Of these, the twin (or the multiple) can be said to be a distinguishing feature of the Nasik-Jorwe culture. Herein we find in a moderate sized pit two grey ware urns with globular profile and wide, flaring rim, placed mouth-to-mouth horizontally and containing, of course, the mortal remains of the departed soul along with burial goods such as vessels of food and water, personal ornaments and tools and weapons [1]. Another variety of this class consists of more than two urns-either three [2] or five [3]-of which two in the middle are placed mouth-to mouth and the others with their mouth accomodating the bottom of the adjoining one in which case the bottom is broken so that all the urns form a sort of coffin. It appears that such urn burials were rather meant for children while the ashes of adults are also occasionally encountered. In the pit burials usually we come across extended skeletons of adults.

The single urn burials form a class by themselves. They are rather rare in the Nasik-Jorwe culture zone and have not so far been encountered anywhere except at Tekwada and Daimabad [4]. Typologically they are altogether different and therefore can be taken to represent, with a reasonable amount of certitude, a different, cultural tradition. Belonging, as they do, to the Nasik-Jorwe culture complex, they appear to be a diagnostic trait of yet a different cultural strain. This would at once become apparent if we take into consideration the fact that the Nasik-Jorwe ware folk at all places preferred the extended or the twin or the multiple urn burial system. Their total absence in the Tekwada cemetery where, at the same time, we come across an entirely different practice of enshrining the mortal remains, brings into relief their unique character and importance. Before, however, assessing the position of these burials *vis-a-vis* other contemporary practices which were in vogue in the Deccan, it is desirable to analyse carefully the evidence from the excavations at Tekwada.

The burials at Tekwada were first discovered by M.N. Deshpande of the Archaeological Survey of India during his explorations of the ancient site at Bahal in 1951, when the stratigraphical horizon of the painted black-on-red pottery, now known as the Jorwe ware, was first determined by H.D. Sankalia and his colleagues in their excavation of the ancient site at Nasik. Bahal, from surface explorations, was established to be a chalcolithic settlement and was therefore selected for stratified excavations. The burial site across the river yielded crude handmade fragments of huge urns and also a black-and-red pottery which can better be described as black-and-grey represented by a variety of bowls reminiscent of those from the Stone Axe culture levels from Brahmagiri. Consequently the Tekwada cemetery was excavated, first in 1952 and again in 1957. We have a brief account of the second season's work [5]. The writer had an opportunity of participating in the Tekwada excavation in 1957. Only a few burials were exposed; they are all quite modest so far as the contents are concerned, but a closer examination will show that they occupy a unique position in the development of chalcolithic cultures as will be evident from the discussion in the following pages which is based mainly on the writer's field observations made during the second season's work.

During the first season in 1952 four burials in all were opened. Of these, three were urn burials and the fourth was a pit burial containing an extended skeleton. The urn burials, on opening, were found to contain, along with the mortal remains, small bowls of the black-and-red or grey ware. The skeleton was deposit ed in a pit specially dug for the purpose and contained a single black-on-red painted vessel of the Nasik-Jorwe fabric. It wast his vessel which instantaneously, and rightly too, led the excavator to correlate the burials with the habitation site of Bahal. In other words, the burials probably represented the mortal remains of the earliest inhabitants of Bahal.

In the second season in 1957 four more burials were excavated. Out of them, three were urn burials, laid in the natural black cotton soil, and fourth, a pit burial cut deep into the underlying yellowish clay. Of the urn burials, one was found disturbed and robbed while the other two were preserved intact. They each consisted of a huge urn covered by a large hemispherical lid and contained a few bones presumably of children and respectively two and five bowls of black-and-red or grey ware. Some of these bowls also bore graffiti,. In one of the jars were found a few beads of paste, a spherical bead of carnelian and a circular, tabular bead of steatite.

The pit burials contained the skeleton of an adult of medium height (about 5 feet 2 inches), laid in a north-south orientation. There were in all three pots in the pit; one of fine grey ware and the other of painted black-and-red variety. The third vessel was a high necked globular jar of the Nasik-Jorwe fabric. It was red slipped and was painted with black. The motif consisted of curvilinear lines forming a shell pattern and joined together by a bank and with six oblique strokes at the top of each curved loop. It was this jar and also the black-and-red pottery which constituted undubitable evidence for connecting the burials with the chalcolithic phase of occupation of Bahal. According to the excavator, the burials are contemporaneous with the phase IB of Bahal [6].

The Tekwada burials are thus modest in form and content and the evidence does appear, on the face of it, quite negligible. But a close analysis of the evidence reveals certain hitherto unknown features. The extended burials have been paralleled at Daimabad [7], but the urn burials are undoubtedly unique for the simple reason that they have no analogues elsewhere [8]. Conversely, the commonest practice of enshrining the mortal remains in twin or multiple urns is conspicuously absent at Tekwada. Instead we have a single urn of different form and fabric, that is, not of the usual grey ware class which is represented at several sites in the Deccan. This typological variation alone would qualify the Tekwada urn burials to be grouped as a class by themselves thus representing an altogether different cultural tradition which is probably betoken of the existence of a new set of people in the chalcolithic population of the Deccan.

The pottery from the burials also merits special attention . The pit burials contained, as reported, a painted black-on-red jar, fine grey ware and painted black-and -red ware pots while the pottery from the urn burials is quite different. The huge urns are of thick, coarse fabric and handmade and are reddish grey in colour. They have an elongated body, ovalloid in shape, with wide flaring mouth, tapering sides and a small flat base. In form and fabric they are entirely different from the usual chalcolithic burial urns which resemble those in the Brahmagiri grey ware. The urns were covered by hemispherical lids of the same fabric. The urns are reported to have contained a number of small black-and-red or grey ware bowls. They were not painted but were scratched with graffiti either on the internal or the external or both the surfaces. They have close analogue in the pottery from the Stone Axe culture phase of Brahmagiri [9] and the shapes also bear a family resemblance to those from megaliths [10]. These bowls contained eatables and water for the deceased.

So far as pottery is concerned, the negative evidence is equally important. In the chalcolithic burials of Maharashtra we usually find painted pottery of the Jorwe fabric and not a single fragment of the black-and-red or grey has so far been found in them. The characteristic spouted vessel and the carinated bowl, both painted, are almost invariably present in the twin or the multiple urn burials. In contradistinction with this, the Tekwada urn burials did not contain a single fragment of any painted vessel which, however, has been reported from the pit burials. The latter in their turn, were also furnished with painted black-and-red ware vessels. It is now known that the painted and the plain black-and-red wares of the proto-historic period are two different ceramic traditions. The absence of the plain black-and-red ware in the pit burials is therefore certainly not without significance. On the whole, the ceramic evidence from the burials tends to point to two different funerary traditions, unrelated to each other.

The stratigraphical evidence should be reasonably expected to provide a convincing proof of the inter-relationship of the pit burials on the one hand and the urn burial on the other. In this connexion it is necessary to impress that the burials lie in the black cotton soil field which has been under cultivation for centuries. Furthermore, they are located on the fringe of the river deposit in such a manner that the monsoonal floods are every year washing away the valuable burial remains and are also disturbing the configuration of the ground. Thus the natural and human agencies have caused unimaginable damage to the cemetery and any attempt at stratigraphy in the excavation of burials was therefore bound to be futile. Nevertheless, an attempt was made to observe the relative stratigraphical position of the two groups of burials. It was noticed that the urn burials were laid in the natural black cotton soil while the burial pit for the extended skeleton was cut deep into the underlying yellowish clay [11]. It is difficult to state precisly what this implies in terms of stratigraphy, but the evidence is certainly not without significance.

Another interesting feature of the Tekwada burials is that they constitute a cemetery by themselves and are not located within the habitation area. In the Nasik-Jorwe culture sites the burials are found within the habitation area itself; more often than not, they are below the house floors [12], a practice which was in vogue in different parts of the world since remotest times. This was done with a view to having the departed soul within the precincts of the house. But the isolation of the cemetery from the habitation as at Tekwada, certainly marks a new development.

Both the pit and the urn burials undoubtedly belonged to the chalcolithic phases for the former is characterised by the evidence of a painted Jorwe ware jar and the latter contained black-and-red pottery similar to that from the Phase I of the habitation. The excavator rightly observes that the burials are contemporaneous with period IB of Bahal [13]. But, if the evidence from the burials—typological, ceramic and stratigraphical—is any indication, it appears that the two different funerary traditions represent two distinct cultural phases, not far removed from each other in point of time. One of them is characterised by painted pottery in the burials while the distinguishing feature of the other, that is, the urn burials is the absence of it. This may superficially appear rather absurd, but has been most unexpectedly corroborated by recent discoveries in Karnatak and Vidarbha.

In the upper Krishna valley of the northern Karnatak a number of neolithic-chalcolithic sites as also innumerable megalithic burials have been recently discovered by A. Sundara [14]. The chalcolithic habitation sites are located along the bank of the river while the megalithic burials are concentrated only in the Kaladgi sandstone zone which is not far from the river course, the maximum distance being about 20 kilometres. The sandstone formations run almost in an east-west direction and as one goes towards east it will be noticed that the Kāladgi rocks and the river gradually come in colse proximity, so much so, that they are both to be seen by the side of each other at Terdal (Bijapur District, Mysore). The place appears to have been of great importance in the ancient past for there are four different localities where relics of the neolithic-chalcolithic period are found while on the adjoining rocky outcrop have been encountered hundreds of megalithic tombs. The small-scale excavation by Sundara revealed that it is a single culture site which was occupied during the neolithic-chalcolithic period which can be equated with the Stone Axe culture of Brahmagiri on the basis of the evidence of the burnished grey ware. It also has, in addition, a painted black-on-red ceramic akin to that from the Tapti valley. The most interesting evidence, from our point of view, comes from a burial of this phase which, curiously enough, situated not within the habitation area but away from it in the locality which was slightly later turned into cemetery by the megalithic people. The burial consisted of an extended inhumation in an ovalloid pit which also contained vessels of the Brahmagiri burnished grey ware fabric, a microlithic outfit and a copper bangle, all of which bear unmistakable affinity with the equipment from the settlement area. The most noteworthy factor here also is the absence of painted pottery in the burial as at Tekwada.

The same story is almost repeated in Vidarbha but in the megalithic context [15]. The excavations at Takalghat and Khapa (both in Nagpur District, Maharashtra) conducted by S.B. Deo on behalf of the Nagpur University have brought to light, for the first time, a habitation at the former site characterised by the use of painted black-on-red pottery associated with black-and-red and micacious wares. The other site, Khapa, is literally strewn with megalithic stone circles which are situated on the other bank of the rivulet,

Krishna by name. The excavation of the burials have yielded a rich range of metal objects buried with human and animal remains. The repertoire of metal objects consists of a variety of tools and weapons of iron and a considerable number of copper objects among which mention should be made of copper mask-like objects with iron rivettings. The burial pottery is the black-and-red ware, the micacious red ware and a coarse red fabric, all exactly similar to those from the habitation site of Takalghat. But surprisingly enough the painted black-on-red pottery, so characteristic of the habitation areas is conspicuously absent in the burials. Deo therefore rightly observes that "if the megalithic builders at Khapa and the inhabitants fo Takalghat were culturally identical, it appears that the painted pottery was used only in everyday life, but not in the burials" [16].

The combined evidence of Takalghat and Khapa is extremely important for it represents a culture which is on the threshold of iron age. The lithic tools are no more required for copper is in use and iron has also at the same time made its advent. The painted pottery tradition too continues. What is important from the point of view of the present study is the absence of painted black-on-red pottery in the burials [17]. It has to be conceded that the megalithic pottery and the burial types have nothing in common with Tekwada urn burials; the only trait that is significant and common to both is the persistent tradition of the use of painted pottery in everyday life but not in burials.

The foregoing analysis of the typological, ceramic, and stratigraphical evidences from the Tekwada burials amply makes it clear that there were two distinct burial traditions in vogue at Tekwada even during the chalcolithic period. They were, in all probability, slightly removed from each other in point of time; the extended inhumations belonging to the heyday of the poineering settlers of Bahal and the urn burials representing the end phase of the chalcolithic period when the black-and-red was coming into its own and the painted pottery tradition was dying out. The same custom was current in in northern Karnatak as the Terdal evidence shows. The tradition further survived at Takalghat and Khapa in Vidarbha in some form or other and it seemd likely that it also influenced the megalithic urn burials of the later period. The megalithic urn of Pudukottai is not typologically far removed from its counterpart at Tekwada [18]. "These are the cultural trends," according to Soundra Rajan, "that we witness in the developing mosaic of habitational and funerary culture diffusion from Central India and Upper Deccan into Lower Deccan, as brought forth by the excavation at Bahal, Ujjain, Maheshwar and Prakash variously to mention only the most significant to yield favourable data in this direction." [19]. The parallels are significant and no doubt lead to the complicated problem of the chronology of megaliths. That, however, is the wider problem of the sub-continent. Presently it would suffice to take into consideration the position of vital importance of the Tekwada burials.

NOTES

[1] *Indian Archaeology* 1958-59, *A Review*, (abbreviated as *IAR*), Pl. XXVA.

[2] Ibid, Pl. XXVB.

[3] *IAR*—1959-60, Pl. XXXB.

[4] This infant-burial is different from that of Tekwada. See *IAR*—1958-59, 18.

[5] *IAR*—1956-57, 18-19.

[6] Ibid, 19.

[7] *IAR*—1958-59, Pl. XXIV A & B.

[8] The Brahmagiri urn burials are of a different category and in no way resemble those of Tekwada. For Brahmagiri types see *Ancient India*, No. 4, 1947-48, Pl. CVIII & CIX.

[9] Ibid, *Cf.* Fig. 21, T 45, 46 a & b ; Fig. 22, bowl types.

[10] Ibid, Fig. 17, bowl types.

[11] *IAR*-1956-57, 18.

[12] H. D. Sankalia and others, *From History to Pre-History at Nevasa*, Poona, 1960, 506.

[13] *IAR*—1956-57, 19.

[14] I am thankful to my friend Sri A. Sundara for the information about the evidence in northern Karnatak which will appear in greater detail in his forthcoming paper entitled 'Preliminary Investigations into the Chalcolithic Phase of the Upper Krishna Valley, North Mysore'.

[15] I am grateful to Prof. S. B. Deo for this information which is based on a brief account circulated by him.

[16] Ibid.

[17] It must only be surreptiously that a painted black-on-red bowl with hole-mouth spout found its way into a megalith at Junapani. See *IAR*-1961-62, 33-34.

[18] V. D. Krishnaswami, 'Megalithic Types in South India', *Ancient India*, No. 5, 1949, Pl. XIVA.

[19] 'Chronological and Cultural Aspects of the Indian Neolithic, Based on Recent Data', *Journal of Indian History*, XLII, 1964, 117.

Stratigraphy, Probable Climatic Phases and Dating of the Stone Age Cultures of Upper Son Valley

by NISAR AHMAD

No palaeontological evidence is yet available from the Son valley to date the various archaeological horizons. However, the river deposits of a few regions in Peninsular India have been dated on palaeontological, geological and archaeological grounds. Hence, against the background of this available evidence, an attempt is made here to work out a chronology of the Stone Age industries and the climatic phases associated with them in the upper Son valley.

Stratigraphy

The river Son, which is parabolic in nature—steep near the source and expanding its bed towards the mouth—exhibits the Pleistocene deposits at Navatola, Salamtola, Bakahi, Ruhanian and Ramnagar—only the last named yields two gravels. Evidently the Pleistocene deposits in this river have been buried under the huge deposits of sands. In Sidhi District, the artifacts come from the loose gravel patches lying on the sand-bed of the stream which are the result of the present aggradation.

That the river is very ancient is proved by the following geomorphological evidences. Near Devalond (24° 12', 61° 20') it twice crosses a prominent ridge of quartzite and the fact is that it had determined its course prior to the existence of this ridge. The east to west course of the Son was established before the formation of the Kaimur scarps when the relief was low and the river flowed over the shales of the soft Lower Vindhyan[1].

However, these evidences of the mainstream were meagre and insufficient to place the various cultures in the proper context and hence the exploration was also carried out in some of its tributaries.

The sequence of various deposits as seen in the river Son and its tributaries is described in the following paragraphs.

Son

The Son rises in the unclassified crystalline archaean formations and after flowing for about 5 km. in the archaean terrain, it flows through Lower Gondwana formations for about 100 km. However, at places it cuts through the trappean outliers during its journey through Lower Gondwana formations. Because of the presence of softer rocks in this part the coarser bouldery and pebbly gravels are not seen in the various cliff sections. And, therefore, at Navatola and Salamtola, which occur in the Lower Gondwana, the bottom of the cliff is composed of highly compact kankars mixed with a few pebbles of quartzite etc. and capped by dark brown sandy silt. The latter is followed by black brown soil. The lower deposit yielded eleven Early Stone Age tools.

After Salamtola, the river was examined at various places. There the banks are composed of yellow brown silt and the river bed is mostly sandy.

At Bakahi and Ruhanian, the sandy gravel patch rests on the rock and is in turn followed by the yellow brown silt and black brown soil, respectively. Late Stone Age tools were picked up from the surface of the black brown soil.

After Markandey the river starts flowing through Upper Vindhyan formations and naturally, because of the change in the bed rock lithology, bouldery and pebbly material is commonly seen in the bed of the river.

In the downstream near Jogadh Bridge, dark brown sandy silt lies over the rock bed and is capped by the sandy gravels, which yielded Middle Stone Age tools. It is followed by yellow brown silt and black brown soil. Early Stone Age tools were obtained from the top of the latter.

At Ramnagar in a rain gully, the cliff-section at the bottom has cemented bouldery and pebbly gravel and is overlain by dark brown sandy silt. It is followed by sandy pebbly gravel and sandy yellow brown silt. On the top is black brown soil. No *in situ* tool could be found in the lower graval. Three MSA tools were discovered *in situ* from the second gravel which is less cemented than the previous one. Two LSA tools were picked up from the surface of the black brown soil.

Katni

On the Kanti *nadi* at Murwara, a well cemented bouldery and pebbly gravel is exposed in the bed of the river and also in the cliff section. It is overlain by highly kankarized silt. The latter deposit is followed by the yellow brown silt and black soil. Seven tools were extracted from the cemented gravel.

The lower cemented gravel and its overlying kankary silt probably represent early Middle Pleistocene, while the yellow brown silt which caps the kankarized silt may belong to late Middle Pleistocene period. No MSA tools could be found either in the Pleistocene deposits or in the modern bed materials of the stream.

Jhepawan

The section on the left bank of river Jhepawan near Banjari shows cemented bouldery and pebbly gravel to be resting on a rock. The gravel is further capped by dark brown silt which is followed by black brown soil. In the gravel layer five ESA tools were found *in situ*.

Hiranya

On the left bank of this *nadi*, near Parnia village, a section, consisted of a well cemented pebbly gravel and followed by dark brown sandy silt, was found. The latter is capped by fairly consolidated sandy gravel which is further overlain by yellow brown silt. On the top is black brown soil. One flake, 160 mm. in length, made on chert, was removed from the pebbly gravel while the overlying sandy gravel yielded two MSA tools made on chert. Two hand-axes made on chert were found in the loose gravel lying in the bed of the stream.

LSA tools were found from the surface of the black brown soil.

Sukha

The section on the left bank of this river near Sidhi town had the deposits of only one period, viz. cemented pebbly gravel and dark brown silt. On the top is black brown soil. No stone age tool could be recovered from the gravel. LSA implements were found from the surface of the black brown soil.

Mohan

On this stream three sections were located, two of them at Deosar and one at Majona. All the three sections show from bottom upwards : cemented pebbly gravel, dark brown silt and black brown soil. One chopper, and one flake were found *in situ* in the gravel at Deosar and Majona respectively. LSA tools were found from the top of the black brown soil at Majona.

Johilla

In the cliff-section of this river between Gorai and Barachanda, slightly cemented bouldery-pebbly gravel rests uncomformably on the Gondwana sandstone. It mainly consists of trap, a few chert and granitic components. This deposit is overlain by sandy brown calcareous silt which is again capped by a thick deposit of slightly cemented pebbly sandy gravel, which in composition and texture does not differ much from gravel I. At places it is more sandy and shows cross-bedding. Both the gravels yield MSA tools made on chert. However, one chopping-tool of chert was also found *in situ* in gravel I. Seven ESA tools made on chert and breccia were collected from the loose gravel bed of the stream within a distance of about 3 km. downstream from this section. LSA tools were picked up from the fields. The overlying silt of gravel II is thick, sandy and calcareous. The intervening silt between gravel I and gravel II does not appear to form a continuous deposit for a considerable distance, instead it thins down within a distance of about 1 km.

From the archaeological as well as geological evidences, it appears that the gravels I and II, observed in the section, are the result of one aggradational phase with slight change in the sedimentation process as represented by intervening silt.

This unusual thick deposition might have occurred because of the sudden drop in the gradient of a river and its feeding tributaries and also because of some obstruction in the form of hard rock barrier which prevented the main stream in carrying its load further downstream. The sandy and silty layers in this gravel deposit mostly indicate channel changes due to braiding and meandering processes.

Summary

The above observations reveal that the deposition of two gravels in the upper Son valley is seen only at Ramnagar (Son) and Parnia (Hiranya). ESA tools could not be found from the basal gravel of Ramnagar and a big flake of chert removed from the lower gravel of Parnia does not provide much support for the existence of ESA industry in that deposit. However, these lower gravels may be equated with the well cemented gravel of Murna (Katni), Deosar, Majona (Mohan) and Banjari (Jhepawan) yielding only ESA tools.

Thus the two periods of aggradation may be noticed in the Pleistocene deposits of the upper Son valley. The ESA bearing gravel is generally bouldery and pebbly in nature and rests uncomformably on the solid rock. It is sometimes capped by sandy dark brown silt. This silt is further capped by MSA bearing sandy gravel which is again overlain by brownish yellow silt.

LSA tools were lying at many places on the top of the black brown soil. It may also be pointed out here that a microlithic industry also had its extension on the lower hills.

Climate

The upper Son receives on an average about 50" of annual rainfall and is fairly covered with open decidurous forest. Tectonically, the region is stable and probably it was so even during the Pleistocene times. The beahviour of the Son is directly not affected by eustatic changes of the Pleistocene. And hence the changes in the nature of the texture of the Pleistocene sediments appear to have occurred mainly because of the climatic changes in the Pleistocene.

The climate in general must have been of the present character, i.e. sub-tropical monsoonic. However, the extensive glaciation in the higher latitudes and also in the Himalayas might have affected the atmospheric circulatory patterns, the rate of evaporation of the sea water etc. and hence this part of peninsular India might have experienced different types of climate during the Pleistocene. There might have been wetter monsoons and drier monsoons probably corresponding with glacial, interglacial fluctuations of the higher latitudes. Whether the changes in the higher and lower latitudes were homotaxical or not, is very difficult to assess in our present state of knowledge of the Pleistocene climate.

Hypothetically, we may assume that the wet period in the upper Son was slightly wetter than the present one and the dry one was much drier than the present one. Both the periods were probably of sufficient duration and intensity so as to affect vegetation and geomorphic processes significantly.

During the wet period, the vegetation cover in the valley probably might have been quite thick as to reduce the surface run off of rain water and also soil stripping. The major streams like the Son were flowing with ample water with increased competence and capacity which enabled them to transport cobbles and pebbles for considerable distances. The rapidly flowing turbulent waters with their powerful tools of pebbles and cobbles of hard quartzites could also eat down vertically their own valleys. The vertical incision as well as deposition of coarser material at suitable places in the channel of the streams must be occurring during even monsoon season in the wet phase. But the overall incision was dominant in the peak period of wet phase while overall deposition of cobbly and bouldery gravels probably ensued during the declining period of wet phase when the capacity and competence along with total discharge of the streams were greatly reduced.

In the dry period, the vegetation matt in the valley probably was very sparse and this increased the surface run off and soil stripping. Lot of finer materials like sand and silt came down into the trunk stream through ill-defined drainage during occasional stormy rains. The competence of the streams was less and the general tendency was more towards aggradation and hence there was general alluviation in the valley—both in the mainstreams and its tributaries—during occasional stormy rains of the dry monsoons.

There were probably two wet phases and two dry phases in the Pleistocene period. In the wet phase, coarse cobbly and pebbly gravels, along with ESA tools were laid down over highly contorted rocky bed. It was followed by a dry phase in which river alluviated its valley with finer sand and silt in which no stone age tools were found.

The second wet phase was probably less intense than the first one and the incision of the earlier alluvium was not very strong and the gravels deposited over the earlier silt in the declining stages of the wet phase were much finer in texture and contain MSA tools.

In the second dry phase the rivers aggraded their beds to the height of about 45 metres from the present water level with very fine silt.

Probably the present climatic phase ensued at the beginning of the Holocene period, the early part of which was much humid. The country got covered with good vegetation and the silt of the second dry phase weathered into black brown soil. The LSA tools occur on the surface of this soil.

Dating

In the peninsular part of India, ESA tools are found along with the Middle Pleistocene fossil fauna, hence they are dated to the Middle Pleistocene [1]. The assemblage included well trimmed handaxes and cleavers along with crudely trimmed specimens and pebble tools. This industry, following the principle of archaeological dating that 'an assemblage should be dated by the most advanced tools rather than by more numerous primitive tools', can be attributed to the level where Acheulian handaxes appeared by the introduction of a new technique—'cylinder hammer'. The well made Acheulian handaxes along with cleavers having a biconvex cross-section and not a parallelogram appeared in East Africa at Olduvai Gorge in stage VII found from the base of Bed IV. The cleavers with parallelogramatic cross-section come there in stage VIII [2]. The ESA industry of India which consists of cleavers, suggests " the direct spread of Acheulian tradition from Africa into India "[3]. The cleavers of parallelogrammatic cross-section indicate that ESA culture in India entered at the Stage VIII of the Olduvai Gorge. Thc Bed IV of the Olduvai Gorge is dated to the upper part of the Middle Pleistocene[4]. Hencc it might be held that in India the ESA culture came in the upper part of the Middle Pleistocene or after that. Wainwright [5], who adopted the method of beginning with modern deposits and working back into the past, has dated the Acheulian tool bearing ESA gravel of Lower Narmada in Gujarat to the last Inter-glacial. Again, in the Potwar region the first assemblage of handaxes is dated to the late Middle Pleistocene [6]. Thus it seems more factual that the ESA culture in peninsular India entered the late or upper Middle Pleistocene or even at the end.

The occurrence of Abbevillian hand-axes and pebble tools along with fine Acheulian hand-axes suggest the survival of the old elements and techniques along with evolved technique.

MSA tools are also found in association with the Middle Pleistocene fossil fauna from the second gravel of the Godavari[7] and the Narmada [8]. However, it is likely that the fossil fauna of this gravel was late survival and therefore, it must be attributed to the upper Pleistocene, or according to our method of calculation late in the upper Pleistocene This industry might have evolved from the earlier culture.

LSA tools come from the surface of the river banks and the hills. They may belong to Holocene because of their association with the black soil.

NOTES

[1] Lake Philip, *Physical Geography*, Edition for India, 1959, 353.

[2] H. D. Sankalia, S. B. Deo, Z. D. Ansari and S. Erhardt, *From History to Pre-History at Nevasa*, 1960, 75-6; H. De Terra and Paterson, *Studies on the Ice Age in India and Associated Human Cultures*, 1939, 313-26.

[3] L.S.B. Leakey, *Olduvai Gorge*, 1951, 106. 117-120.

[4] K. P. Oakley, *Frameworks for Dating Fossil Man*, 1964, 224.

[5] L. S. B. Leakey, *Olduvai Gorge*, 1951-61, I, 1965, 43.

[6] G. J. Wainwright, *The Pleistocene Deposits of the Lower Narmada River and an Early Stone Age Industry from the River Chambal*, 44-45.

[7] T. T. Paterson and H. J. H. Drummond, *Soan, the Palaeolithic of Pakistan*, 1962, 95.

[8] *Op. cit.* [2], 105.

[9] *IAR*—1958-59, 27.

Megalithic Remains in the Aravallis

by PURUSHOTTAM SINGH

It was more than a century ago when Carlleyle reported megalithic graves from the northern fringes of the Aravallis. However, it was during the last two decades that their importance was emphasised, although no field work was done to ascertain their exact nature. Now that a few of the megaliths of the Kaimur ranges have been systematically excavated, it has become imperative to study similar monuments in the Aravallis in the light of this newly obtained data. With this idea in the mind the author explored the megalithic sites of Khera, Satmas and Daosa and noted their features besides collecting their photographic record.

Khera

The first group of megalithic monuments has been located in the Fatehpur Sikri range of the Aravallis. Here, seven cairns were located by Carlleyle [1] on the ridge of a hill at a little distance to the north-east of Khera, a village situated on the face of the hill, about 4 miles to the west of Fatehpur Sikri. He typologically divided these cairns in two categories, viz. flat-topped cairns and round topped cairns. In two round-topped cairns he found shallow, oblong trough-shaped cavity, roughly excavated in the solid rock of the hill. These contained a layer of pale-coloured earth or fine yellowish sand foreign to the locality. Below this layer of earth or sand, he found the grey dust of the ashes of calcined bones mixed with earth and a few small fragments of charred wood.

In another cairn of the flat-topped variety, he found a small square chamber. The chamber was found filled with stone rubbles and at the bottom was found the grey dust possibly of calcined bones mixed with earth and small atoms of charcoal.

In a recent visit, the present author located the seven cairns (Pl. VA) on the hill mentioned above. These cairns have an average diameter of 2.90 metres [2] and they rise to a height of nearly one metre above the surrounding rock-surface. The author was struck by the comparative freshness of the stone-rubbles used in those cairns (Pl. VB). If surface weathering of these rubble stones is any index to their antiquity, then the Khera cairns may prove to be of recent origin in comparison to those of Satmas and Daosa. However, much spade-work has to precede before such a relative chronology can finally be established.

Satmas

The next group of megalithic remains was located on the Satmas [3] hill at a distance of two miles to the north-east of Jagner which is situated at a distance of about 36 miles to the south-west of Agra and 18 miles to the south of Fatehpur Sikri. Here again, Carlleyle [4] had located a number of cairns or heaps of stones well over a century ago. He counted nearly thirty cairns on the slope of the hill, besides others, on the ridge of the hill. Some of these cairns were opened by him who typologically classified them in three categories.

1. Round-Topped or tumulus-shaped solid cairn below the level of which a shallow sepulchral trough had been excavated in the rock.
2. Flat-topped four-sided cairn containing a small square chamber at the bottom of

A. Khera : General view of the cairns on the western slope of the hill.

B. Khera : Close-up of a cairn.

A. Satmas : Close-up of a huge cairn.

B. Satmas : A rectangular enclosure made of upright stone blocks.

the mass, but always in the body of the cairn and above ground.

3. Cromlech cairn. It contains a rectangular chamber within it, like a cromlech, only the walls are composed of loose rubble stones instead of slabs. Beneath this, a sepulchral chamber is hollowed out in the rock surface which is sometimes filled with small stones.

These three types of cairns differed in their size as well as in their methods of construction. The round-topped cairns generally measured 10 to 12 ft. in diameter. The chamber in the interior of the cairns was very small and if a complete skeleton had to be interred, it would necessitate the doubling up of a corpse in squatting position. The mean diameter of cromlech cairns is 6'6" ×4' to 5'. These are 4'6" in height. The bodies were interred either whole or in fragments after cremation. Thus while flat-topped cairns yielded only small atoms of bones mixed with ashes, the round-topped cairns and cromlechs yielded a few fragile fragments of bones *in situ*. Carlleyle maintains that post-cremation burial as well as complete burial was in vogue at this place.

Besides the three types of monuments noted by Carlleyle, the present author, while on a visit to the site, located yet another type of monument. It consists of a small cist made of four stone slabs without any other lithic appendage (Pl. VIB). However, only one example of this variety was noted on the slope of the hill. An excavation of this type of monument of this site to throw valuable light on the mode of burial should be carried out.

Daosa

Another megalithic site of considerable importance is Daosa (Deosa), situated about 32 miles east of Jaipur on Jaipur-Agra road. Carlleyle had reported three types of monuments at this site. These are :—

1. Stone circles with a cromlech or a menhir in the centre.
2. Cairns and
3. Rude monolith.

Of these, the first group of monuments were located on the gently sloping ground to the north of the foot of the hill. The diameter of these four stone circles varies between 25 ft. to 16 ft. Some of the stone boulders were still in position [6] when Carlleyle visited this site almost a century ago. These boulders measured 3 to 4 ft. in height. One of these stone circles had a ' perfect cromlech ' in its centre. This cromlech was 6 ft. square and rose to a height of 4 ft. Its four walls were composed of 4 rough slabs of stone. The top of this cromlech was imperfectly covered by two narrow slabs of stone laid on and across it. The other two circles had monoliths or menhirs in the centre. Of these, one monolith was of considerable size, as it measured 21 ft. in length and 2 ft. in thickness. The monolith in the second circle was only 5 ft. in height. The fourth circle of stones did not contain any other monument in its centre. These cricles of stones were not subjected to excavation hence their precise nature could not be ascertained.

The second type of megaliths included several cairns situated to the north-east of Daosa village. Some of the cairns were opened by Carlleyle who found a few fragments of calcined human bones and a little charcoal and ashes thus establishing their sepulchral nature. The stone implements obtained from these cairns included a stone knife or dagger, a rude borer-like implement and a stone ball.

The third type of monument included a solitary rude stone monolith measuring 15 ft. ×4 ft. ×2 ft. and was still standing erect at a short distance to the west north-west of Daosa village. But no excavation was carried out at its base hence its exact nature could not be ascertained. The present author's work at Daosa revealed that two types of monuments, viz. cairns and a menhir

(Pl. VII) can still be seen on the site. The author located more than half a dozen cairns on the eastern slope of the outcrop situated on the south-eastern fringes of the modern Daosa town. The latter class of monument was represented by a solitary specimen (Pl. VII B). Other monuments mentioned by Carlleyle seem to have now been destroyed by the sprawling dimensions of the new Daosa town and its populace. Another noteworthy feature of this site is the occurrence of a few pottery sherds. The author was able to collect a few pieces of an ill-fired red ware from the vicinity of the cairns. Here it may also be mentioned that earlier explorers have reported cairns and cinerary urns from other places also in this range. Thus seme stone circles were seen by Garrick [7] at Kuchera near Nagaur and some cinerary urns containing human bones were discovered by Carlleyle [8] at the base of two large boulders in front of the rock which bears the Asokan inscription at Bairat. Besides an aboriginal tomb has been reported from the summit of a lofty range of hills at Machari[9] situated about 22 miles to the south of Alwar.

As has been pointed out earlier, the importance of the megalithic remains in the Aravallis was first of all realized by Wheeler [10]. That the cairns of the Aravallis are associated with the cult of the dead is amply clear by the description given by Carlleyle who has also recorded a tradition [11] about the construction of these graves. It says that these cairns mark the place where members of a royal marriage party were killed in ancient times by natural agencies like thunderbolts, lightning etc. or by decoits. Similar legends about these cairns has also been recorded by James Tod [12]. Here it is worthwhile to record that the Bhil of this region raise cairns over the graves of their dead even today.

Various types of megaliths have been reported from north-western India, Kashmir, Sind and Baluchistan. The importance of the megaliths of Aravallis lies in the fact that these are situated midway between the megalithic graves of the Vindhyan ranges of the one hand and Baluchistan on the other. Lastly, it may be pointed out that local people of this region are quarrying and destroying the rubbles on the hills of Satmas and Khera and there may not remain any trace of these graves after a few years. Therefore, an early excavation and study of these graves is a desideratum.

NOTES

[1] A.C.L. Carlleyle, 'Report on a Tour in East Rajputana in 1871-72 and 1972-73' *Rep. Arch. Surv. Ind.* VI, (1878), 13.

[2] Carlleyle notes that two or three of these cairns measured more than 10 ft. in diameter. However, the author could not locate any cairn with a diameter of over 10 ft.

[3] A.C.L. Carlleyle, 'Report on Agra', *Rep. Arch. Surv. Ind.*, IV, (Calcutta : 1878), 213-14.

[4] A.C.L. Carlleyle, 'Report of a Tour in Eastern Rajput na', *Rep. Arch. Surv. Ind.* VI, (Calcut a 1978), 33-39.

[5] A.C.L. Carlleyle, 'Report of a Tour in Eastern Rajputana'. *Rep. Arch. Surv. Ind.*,*VI* (Calcutta : 1878).

[6] As reported by Carlleyle. In a recent visit to the site the present author could not locate any circle of stone except a solitary menhir measuring nearly 3 ft. above ground

[7] H.B.W. Garrick, 'Report of a Tour in Punjab and Rajputana in 1883-84', *Rep. Arch. Surv. Ind.*, XXII, 1887, 49-50.

[8] A.C.L. Carlleyle, *Rep. Arch. Surv. Ind.*, VI, (Calcutta : 1878), 100-101.

[9] A.C.L. Carlleyle, *Rep. Arch. Surv. Ind.*, VI, 88-89.

[10] R.E.M. Wheeler, 'Brahmagiri and Chandravalli : 1947', *Ancient India*, No. 4, 302 ff.

[11] A.C.L. Carlleyle, *Rep. Arch. Surv. Ind.*, IV, 214. Also Carlleyle, *Rep. Arch. Surv. Ind.*, VI, 33-39.

[12[James Tod, *Travels in Eastern India*. 30. Also his, *Annals and Antiquities of Rajasthan*, 648.

A. Daosa : General view of the cairns on the eastern slope of the hillock.

B. Daosa : Close view of the solitary menhir.

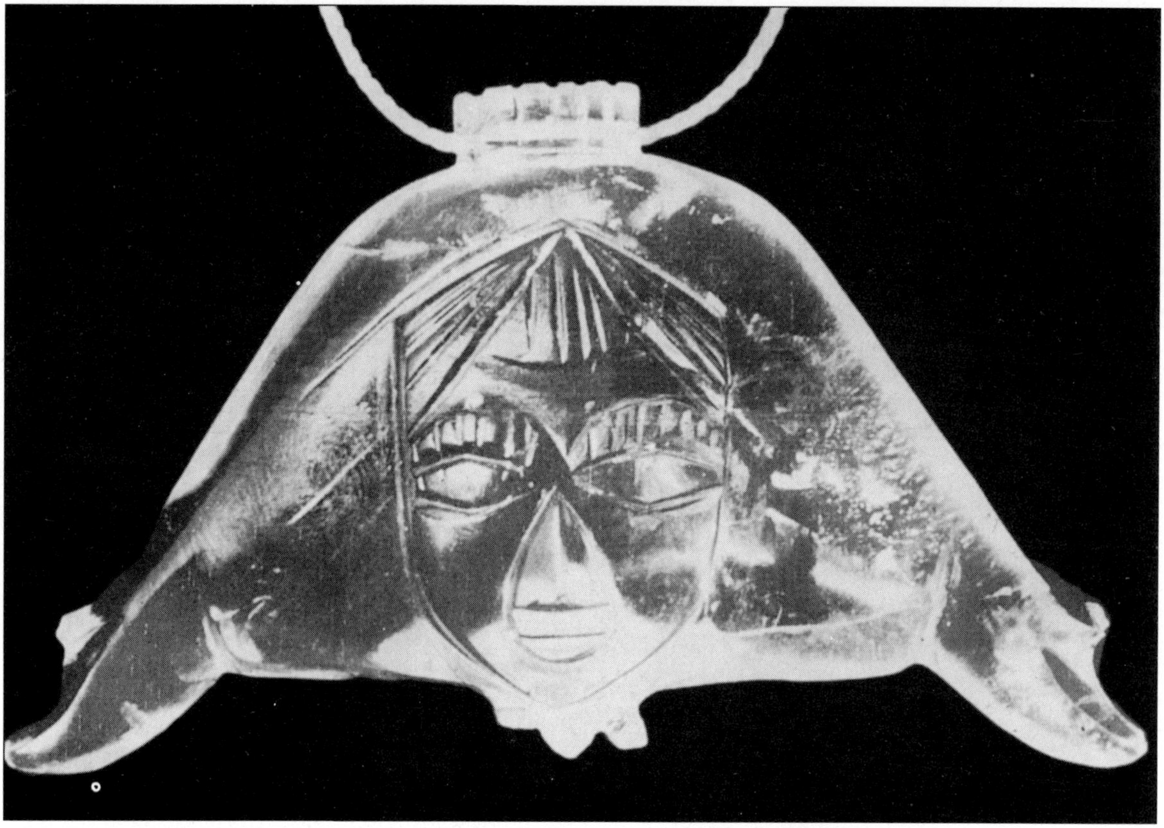

Crystal pendant from Rajghat.

Three Crystal Pendants of Identical Design

by P. K. AGRAWALA

Quartz crystal is a precious stone which has been widely used for making various artistic shapes and objects of aristocratic utility since chalcolithic ages. Here we wish to draw the attention of scholars to three crystal pendants discovered at Bhita, Rajghat and Sonpur. It is a striking fact that all the three pieces found from various sites show an identical design. They are so similar to each other that from the photographs one may be confused for the other if not examined with a great precising eye for minute details. The high attainments of Indian lapidarist's art are fully testified from these pieces which display a skilful mastery in cutting hard stones like crystal with so much precision and the intricate designing of a remarkably stylised figure to be seen on them no doubt characterises a highly developed art.

Of the three pieces, the one from Bhita was first to be discovered. It was found in the excavations done on this site by John Marshall in 1911-12 [1]. According to his description, it is a crystal pendant of Gupta date, with human face roughly incised on one side, and found from the trial trench 43 [2]. No further details are given by him as to its size and other characterising features which one would expect for this valuable piece. His dating of the object also seems to be just 'customary' and without much reference as to its stratigraphic associatoins and nothing of stylistic sequence we can know from his report about the trench 43 except a few beads and the bricks of a crude structure which provide no hints to any specific dating.

The other pendant similar to the Bhita one is now in the Bharat Kala Bhavan. It is said to have come from Rajghat and was purchased from a local dealer. It has already been published by Dr. Moti Chandra in his *Kāshī kā Itihāsa* (Fig. 4, facing p. 80) with a caption saying, 'A female head, cut in crystal ; Śuṅga Period, B. C. 2nd century, Rajghat (Bharat Kala Bhavan).' We are thankful to the Director of Bharat Kala Bhavan for allowing us to have a photograph of it which is being reproduced here with due courtesy.

The third identical piece of this class has been recently found from the Sonpur excavations (1961-62), first published in the *Indian Archaeology* 1961-62—*A Review* [3] and also being described here along with a photograph by Dr. B. P. Sinha. It comes from Period II, datable roughly to B. C. 600—B. C. 200.

All these strikingly similar pieces have horizontal perforations on the upper portion in which a thread can be pierced. They are illustrated here as such on plates VIII & IX A & B. This shows beyond doubt their use as pendant and presumably they were worn in the neck as pectorals and as forming charm against evil. The upper projection bearing sidewise holes for the thread is beautified in all the three instances with the dentil motif.

An almost identical human face is to be seen on them. It represents a masterful sketch of the facial outline executed by incisions. It is rectilinear or somewhat rhomboid in shape. The hair is shown with suggestive scratches as meeting in the middle of the head and with a braid in the centre covering the forehead above the eyebrows which makes an impressive design for its contrast with the incised lines slanting inward from the two sides. The eyes are rendered with two arches for the eye-brows and with two diamond-shaped patterns representing eye balls. The nose and mouth together are shown by a leaf-design placed with its taper upwards reaching the centre of the eyes. The effective stylised rendition of the human face is no doubt of outstanding merit.

Moti Chandra thinks [4] that the figure represents a female. Though there are no decisive indications in its figuration, a few arguments can be given as to its identity as a female. The arrangement of hair may suggest that it is a female shown which the parting of hair in the middle (*sīmanta*) as has been the fashion for an Indian lady blessed with *saubhāgya*. Further, an effiminate expression is to be observed in the rendition of the face which strikes in all the three examples. Whether the representation was intended to be that of a goddess or some female divinity of a lower status will be extremely doubtful if suggested.

Another striking feature of these objects are the two projections on either side of the lower portion. They appear as if pointed fangs of an animal, possibly of a tiger, were suggested by the artist. From examining the original specimen of the Bharat Kala Bhavan, we can say that there is hardly any thing which would lead us to identify some particular shape. They are simply fashioned as two pointed projections which may stand for tiger's fangs or claws or something similar. But their presence invariably in all the three instances appears to be with some specific intention by their artists.

No doubt, in Gupta inconography we find such details as flanking a pectoral worn by the certain Kārttkeya and Kṛishṇa images [5]. The ornament to be seen on the chest of these deities consists of a central round pendant enclosed between two nail-like things on either side. We are sure as to its identification. This type of amulet is still current as an efficacious charm worn round the neck of children and known as *baghanak* ('claw of the tiger') [6]. The projections to be seen in the crystal pendants possibly refer to the same type of representation. If so, their purpose as symbols of beatific nature will be significant. The practice of enclosing a central symbol by two flanking motifs can be traced back to the Śuṅga period. On the chest of a Yakshī [7], (labelled as *Cha(ṁ)dā Yakhī*) from Bharhut, the torque worn round the neck displays in the centre a *śrīvatsa* which is flanked on either side by two spike-shaped symbols. Though the identity of the lower side projections in the crystal pendants with these spike-shaped (or *aṅkuśa*) symbols on the chest of the Yakshī, cannot be argued, yet a similar suggestivity appears to have been in both the cases.

From the three crystal pendants under discussion, we have an idea how a motif of art was widely circulated over an extended territory as they were found separately from the excavations at different sites at various occasions. They appear as if 'cast from the same mould', if at all we are allowed to use this phrase for the pieces cut in crystal. They are so identical to each other (except their size) that one is provoked to have a view that they were possibly the works of a single artist and were exported to various distant places.

NOTES

[1] *Annual Report, ASI,* 1911-12, Calcutta, 1915, Pl. XXXII, 9.

[2] Ibid. 94.

[3] *I. A.* R.—1961-62, New Delhi, 1964, 4 Pl. IVA.

[4] Moti Chandra, *Kashi ka itihasa*, Bombay, 1962.

[5] Seated Karttikeya and Govardhanadhari Krishna, Bharat Kala Bhavan. Also see my *Skand-Karttikeya—a Study in Origin and Development*, Varanasi, 1968, 80-2, and Pls. XVII b; also XVII a, XVIII a & XIX b.

[6] Ibid, 80-2.

[7] Illustrated by Dr. V. S. Agrawala in his *Studies in Indian Art*, Varanasi, 1965, Pl. III.

Crystal Human-Figure From Sonepur

by B. P. SINHA

Rock-crystal is a semi-precious quartz stone. In India its chief find-spots are Tanjore, Kalabagh, Kashmir and a few other places, where crystalline quartz of the requisite purity are obtained [1]. A leading authority has observed that the Alps and India are supposed to have furnished the ancients with their supplies of rock crystal[2]. From Jankara in Kathiawar, the bed of the Godavari near Rajmahendri, the stream beds of Tanjore and formerly even Delhi region, crystal prisms were obtained. Small bi-pyramidal cyrstals have been obtained from marls of the Mari in the Mianwali district of the Punjab, and are known as Mari diamonds.

Objects made of crystal have been in use in ancient India from the Neolithic times. Microliths made of rock cyrstal were noticed at Nagarjunakonda [3], Brahmagiri, and at later place continued in the early phase of the megalithic culture. In the Harappan culture crystal beads were manufactured. At Mohenjodaro a few short barrel-shaped and at Harappa one globular crystal bead were found [4]. The occurrence of lump of crystal ready to be cut for beads at Chanhudaro [5] shows that crystal beads were manufactured locally here. The occurrence of only one perforated short bead at Rangpur III [6] associated with lustrous Red Ware tends to suggest that crystal bead making was not much popular in post-Harappan chalcolithic cultures of western and central India. In the Black-and-Red Ware chalcolithic complex at Oriup (Bihar), were found a few cyrstal beads. Those have to be dated latest before 6th century B.C. In Jaugada, District Ganjam, crystal beads with Black-and-Red Ware (Period-I) but associated with iron may be noted [7].

With the emergence of NBP, use of crystal products becomes again popular. From Hastinapura were found in Period III (NBP) crystal beads, and one pyramidal shaped pendant from Period IV [8]. Crystal beads of Period II (NBP) from Ujjain, and from NBP levels of Vaiśāli may be noted [9]. Taxila yielded a large number and of a variety of crystal objects. NBP stratum (IV) at Bhir mound yielded a star of highly polished crystal [10]. Crystal beads were manufactured in all periods in Taxila.

However, a unique crystal object, in course of excavations, was discovered at Sonepur in the Gaya district in Bihar in the NBP stratum (Period II) [11]. This is a tiny human face of a female, well-finished (slightly damaged on the right side), horizontally perforated on the top of the head. This was probably used as a pendant. What does the figure indicate ? This can only be speculated. It must have had some religious or magical significance. It may be of some interest to know that in Bihar even today a married woman, who is the second wife (after the death of the first wife) of a husband has a stone pendant or a metal (silver) pendant hanging on her chest, probably as a mark of respect to the dead co-wife, or to ward off any evil from her spirit.

The artistic quality of this crystal piece has to be noted. The depiction of the eyes and eye-brows, and the very proportionate figure of the face with porminent nose and lips have been beautifully cut into the hard rock. We get an idea of the hair-dress of the longish faced woman. The extension on the both sides from the head of the figure suggests that the head of the woman was covered by *odhani* like thing. Thus some idea about the dress of the time may be also obtained.

But the importance of the figure lies in its being so far the only known example of its kind for such an early period. We do not know any such or similar crystal human-figure having been found in stratified layer belonging to the NBP period. That the art of the stone-cutter had reached the same degree of excellence as that of the potter in the period in Bihar is a legitimate conclusion.

NOTES

[1] D. N. Wadia, *Geology of India*, London, 493.

[2] J. Marshall, *Mohenjodaro and the Indus Civilization*, II, London, 1931, 678.

[3] *Indian Archaeology*, 1958-59, 5, 1959-60, 6.

[4] *Ancient India*, No. 4, 252.

[5] E. Mackay, *Chanhudaro Excavations*, 1935-36, 209.

[6] *A. I.* No. 18-19, 144, Fig. 52, Pl. XXXIV—4.

[7] *I.A.*R. 1956-57, 30.

[8] *A. I.* No. 10-11, 92-94, Fig. 29.

[9] *I.A.*R. 1957-58, 36; Krishna Deva, *Vaisali Excavations*, 62, Pl. XXIV, No. 17.

[10] J. Marshall, *Taxila*, I, 102.

[11] *I. A.*R., 1961-62, 4.

A. Crystal pendant from Bhitra.

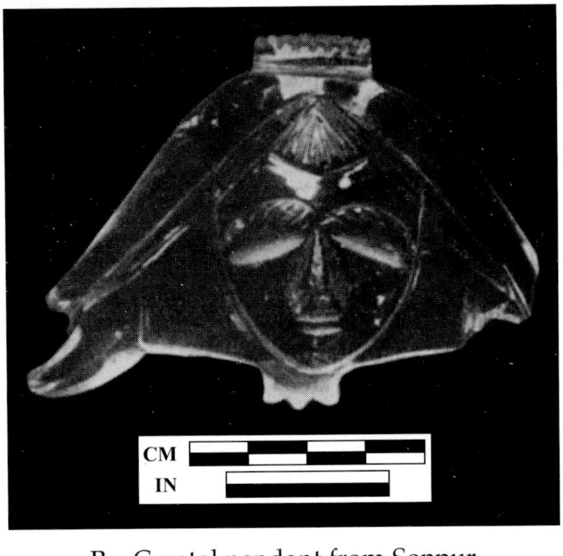

B. Crystal pendant from Sonpur.

C. Sealing from Musnagar.

A

B

C

D

Śiva-linga from Nānda. The lowest figures in A, B, C, D are those of *Viṣṇu*, *Ekanaṁsa* or *Lakṣmī*, *Vāsudeva* and *Baladeva* with a plough, respectively.

Chaturmukha Siva-Linga from Nānd, near Pushkar, Rajasthan

by R.C. AGRAWALA,

This is to discuss the important discovrey of a life-size and four faced Śiva-*liṅga* in white spotted red sand stone. Under worship in a field at Nand, near Pushkar in district Ajmer of Rajasthan, it was briefly noticed by me in the B.C. Bhattacharya Volume of the *Journal of Oriental Institute*, Baroda, Vol. XIV, 1965, pp. 388-391. The colossal *liṅga*, datable to 2nd century A.D., was excavated further and it revealed very unusual iconographic peculiarities. It is carved in four horizontal tiers, on each of the four sides facing the four cardinal directions. The lowest portion represents *Vishṇu Bhāga* so as to depict carvings of Vishṇu (Pl. XA), goddess *Ekānaṁśā* (Pl. XB) along with Vāsudeva and Baladeva (Pl. XC&D). Further up may be identified portions representing Brahmā (?), Sūrya and śiva respectively on all the four sides; they are somewhat mutilated. One one side of Sūrya portion, we even find the male deity (i.e. Sun) putting on a Scythian type of conical cap on his head and lotus stalk in the right hand (Pl. XB.). The topmost portion of this *liṅga* is now covered, on four sides, with headless representation of *ūrdhvaretas* Lakulīśa, seated in squattish pose as also evident in most of the Kushāṇa sculptures from Mathura. The impact of Kushāṇa art traditions on this *liṇga* is further confirmed by the carvings of typical Kushāṇa type of crowns and right hands raised up in *abhaya* pose, in most of the male figures and, on all the four sides of the pillar like *liṇga* under review. This is how it reflects the syncronism of Brahmā-Vishṇu-Sūrya and Śiva in one at such an early stage. The squattish pose for Lakulīśa on all sides of Nānd *Liṅga* above is also interesting and important.

The Śiva-*Liṅga* from Nānd, in Rajasthan, is decidedly an important relic in the realm of early Indian art. Another specimen of this type has not been discovered as yet. In the Nānd-*liṅga*, under review, we notice all the figures as emanating from those carved in the lowest panel as also in the *Viśvarūpa* Vishṇu from Bharat Kala Bhavan, Varanasi. The former is quite different from the contempory four-faced-*liṇgas* of Mathura art and preserved in the National Museum [2] at New Delhi and Municipal Museum at Allahabad.[3]

Even the famous Bhīṭā-*liṅga*, now exhibited in State Museum at Lucknow, fails to present the details represented by the column-like *liṅga* from Nand, in Rajasthan. It is therefore evident that there did exist various types of Śiva-*liṅgas* during the Kushāṇa period. Elsewhere, in one specimen from Mathura itself, we notice only four-armed Śiva standing against the column-like phallus and twisting his matted locks round it with his raised up upper hands.[4]

The aforesaid column like *lıṇga* from Nānd thus appears to depict the earliest extant form of four-faced Śiva-Liṅgas which may present the blending of four principal Brahmanic deities into one; it may well be regarded as the predecessor of *Śiva-liṇgas* of early-mediaeval and mediaeval periods. Lakullṇa was later on substituted by four Śiva-heads on top of the *liṅgas* whereas standing figures of Brahmā, Vishṇu, Sūrya and

Śiva came to occupy the remaining portions of the same *liṅga* as in a 7-8th century *Chaturmukha-Liṅga* from Kalyāṇpur[5] (Rajasthan) and elsewhere.

The Nānd *Liṅga* has also got an important bearing on the antiquity of Lakulīśa cult in Rajasthan. Here we notice only the figures of Lakulīśa[6] on all the four sides above; he is shown as seated in the squattish pose which was quite popular at Mathura during the Kushāṇa period. Later on, we come across Lakulīśa usually in *pādmasana* [7] pose as in the sculptural art of Western India. Independent images of squattish or seated Lakulīśa as such are of course yet to be discovered in the realm of Kushāṇa art though we do some across a number of Kushāṇa carvings of *ūrdhvaretas* Śiva from Mathura and its vicinity. Viewed in this light, the aforesaid Śiva-*liṅga* from Nānd is really of great interest for the students and scholars of ancient Indian iconography and cultural history. It is hoped that expertsof Indian art and literatuer will throw more light on some of the important and unusual iconographic features represented therein. It is in fact a very rare specimen in the domain of early Indian art.

NOTES

[1] Photographs have been prepared by Mr. Vijaya Kumar and kindly supplied by the Director, Archaeology & Museums, Rajasthan., Jaipur. I am thankful to Dr. Satya Prakash as well.

[2] Published by R.C. Agrawala in *East & West*, Rome, XVII, (3-4), 1967, 276, figures 1-2.

[3] An unpublished specimen.

[4] A. Coomaraswamy, *History of Indian & Indonesian Art*, London, 1927, figure 68; R. Sen Gupta's paper in *JAS*, Calcutta, IV(2), 1962, 41-47, plate IV B. It recalls)o our minds the famo us *linga* from Gudimall am, depicting standing Siva against the phallus in the art of first century B.C.

[5] R.C. Agrawala, *Sculptures from Udaipur Museum*, Jaipur, 1960, Plate XV.

[6] All the heads of *Lakulisa* in this *linga* are completely mutilated. It is therefore difficult to hazard any opinion about the exact nature of Siva heads facing two cardinal directions.

[7] R.C. Agrawala, *Journal of Oriental Institute*, Baroda, XIV, 1965, 388-91 for standing Lakulisa from Western India.

A Neolithic Burial from T. Narasipur

by M. SESHADRI

In the summer of 1961, during the excavation of the ancient site on the left bank of the Cauvery at T. Narasipur Sangam, conducted by the Archaeological Department of Mysore a burial of the Neolithic Culture was uncovered in TN 16 (Pl. XI) well within the habitation area. It is an extended burial in a roughly oblong cradle-shaped pit, having its major axis in the east-west direction. Two post-holes were seen, one on either side of the oblong burial-pit cut into layers 5 and 6 (Pl. XII A). The body was lying on its back, with the head towards east and the crossed hands placed on the abdomen. The face was slightly tilting to the right. The legs were stretched. Two large grey ware pots with globular body and everted rims were placed near the head. These were hand made and slightly burnished. There was also a shallow lipped bowl and a pottery "neck rest" (head-rest) near the head itself. The pit containing the body and the funerary offerings (Pl. XII B) was filled up with the same soil gathered during its digging. There was no stone or any such appendage to indicate the burial pit. The purpose of the post-holes could not be made out.

The skeleton had undergone much post-mortal deterioration. However, a careful study, after reconstruction of the skeleton, by Sri K.C. Malhotra, the Anthropologist of the Deccan College, Post-Graduate Research Institute, Poona, has given sufficient data relating to the racial features. His study has revealed that the skeleton is of a woman aged about 21-25 years belonging to the Mediterranean stock. The individual possesses a medium-sized high-vaulted head, long face, feebly developed supra-orbital ridge and occipital torus, slightly sub-nasal prognathism and medium cranial capacity, i.e., about 1,300 C.C. The stature has been estimated to be about 5'2". The present fiind shows a good deal of similarity with the other neolithic human skeletal remains of the Deccan: Piklihal, Tekkalakota, and Nagarjunakonda. It is possible that the people responsible for the neolithic cultural phase in the Deccan possessed a uniform pheno-type, i.e., Mediterranean and possibly whatever differences are depited are largely due to admixture. How it is different from those of the cholcolithic skeletal series such as Nevasa, Mohenjodaro and Harappa and the megalithic of southern India such as Adichanallur, Brahmagiri, Yeleswaram has to be ascertained.

Some of the modern communities of Karnataka such as the Ādikarnataka, Agasa, Gāniga and Brahmins like the Babburkamme bear certain physical characteristics similar to the T. Narasipur specimen. An examination of the teeth of the present skeletan has revealed that the individual was suffering from caries. This is probably the earliest evidence of the existence of that disease, so common in India today.

On archaeological evidence the present burial is assignable to about the first half of the 2nd millennium B.C.

The T. Narasipur burial presents some features of its own. Majority of the neolithic burials and the chronologically-nearer chalcolithic, extended, adult ones of the Deccan have a north-south orientation unlike the one from T. Narasipur. In many of the burials at Brahmagiri, Nagarjunakonda and Piklihal, a spouted pot is normally associated, but it is absent here. If any libation was poured out, the lipped-bowl was used for that purpose. Apart from the orientation, the attitude and the position of the hands too are somewhat peculiar. The burial, further contains a terracotta 'neck-rest'. The presence, in the burial under study, very near the head (temple) shows that this might have been used as a 'head-rest'. Allchin has already drawn attention to the use of varieties of head-rests in many of the modern primitive communities of South-East Asia and Africa. He has also pointed out that head-rests, almost similar to the T. Narasipur type, were widely in use in the Nile valley right from pre-Dynastic times down to the Roman period. While wood, stone and metal ones were popular, pottery ones, too, are not unknown there.

Pottery head-rests, are hitherto known in India only in the Neolithic of the Cauvery Valley. Can the occurrence of similar ones in the Nile region be a pointer towards the solving of the problems of the origin of the Neolithic Culture of South India?

General view of an excavated trench at T. Narasipur (Mysore).

A. Burial pit with skeleton and pottery at T. Narasipur.

B. Grave-goods associated with the burial from T. Narasipur.

An Interesting Sealing from Musanagar

by KIRAN KUMAR THAPLYAL

The terracotta sealing discussed below comes from Musanagar (80°10′ N. and 79°58′ E.) [1], a small town in Kanpur District, thirty-four miles from Kanpur and now in State Museum, Lucknow [2]. The antiquity of Musanagar as well as its archaeological importance is well known since long [3].

The sealing is of greyish colour and broken on the right side. The extant portion measures 4 cms. in length and 3.5 cms. in width at the maximum points (Pl. IX C). Its original size, however, is a matter of conjecture.

The sealing shows in high relief two bulls standing beside each other and facing right. The one in the foreground covers much of the second figure and is shown either in a belligerent mood or rubbing its head against a tree trunk with the tail slightly raised suggesting excitement. There are some saddle-like marks on the back of the bull recalling to mind the saddles on the back of some of the animals on Harappan seals. The other bull stands placidly facing towards the same direction.

There are two objects—in between the fore and hind legs and another between the two hind ones. The former is domical in shape. If any religious significance is to be attached to it then the object in the context of the bull might stand for a *linga*. Else the two objects may be treated as stones depicted in order to heighten the effect of the landscape.

The part of the seal having the delineation of the trunk of the tree is broken and missing. The way leaves have been depicted above the head of the bull in the foreground gives the impression of a banana tree. Leaves and a flower or fruit [4] have also been shown from the branch above the back of the bull in the background. It may be suggestive of banana leaves and flower or another branch of some tree.

The sealing bears some figure indistinctly drawn on the left of the two bull figures which cannot be positively identified. However, the plausibility of another animal figure facing front cannot be denied.

There is a deep groove lengthwise on the back of this sealing suggesting its use for sealing letters parcels, or documents. Whether the sealing is of local origin or came from outside is difficult to ascertain.

As regards the date of the sealing there is nothing to fall back upon except its stylistic consideration, as it is just a chance discovery. In the museum records it has been ascribed to' C. 5th or 4th century B.C. '[5]. A comparison of this sealing with its counterparts of the historic period tends to show that there is hardly any similarity between the two. The very mode of depicting the two bulls in perspective—one in the foreground and another in the background is a proof of the remarkable skill and understanding on the part of the artist rarely to be seen on the latter ones. Of the bulls it was the humped variety that was favourite of the artists of India throughout its art-history. We may, however, note that taken individually, there is some similarity between the bull and tree figures on the seal and the ones depicted on a few of the Harappan seals [6].

In the present state of our knowledge about the antiquity of the site Musanagar [7], it would be premature to assert with certainty about the protohistoric affinities of this sealing purely on stylistic grounds. Yet we may recollect that the find of a few stray seals in India has been startling in as much as they have been treated as evidentiary links between India on the one hand and Mesopotamia and Crete on the other. The cylinder seal in Central Museum, Nagpur (datable to c. 2,000 B.C.) [8] and a cylinder one from Maski [9] point to Indo-Mesopotamian contacts while a button seal unearthed recently from Pandu Rajar Dhibi (West Bengal) has been taken to suggest Indo-Cretan contacts in the second millennium B. C.[10]. Recent explorations and excavations have widened the extent of Harappa culture considerably. Now when Harappa culture has been traced at Alamgirpur (District Meerut) and even further east and Harappan traits have been suspected at Kausāmbī, if a seal suggestive of protohistoric affinities is found at Musanagar, the find should appear less startling than the ones enumerated above.

The belligerent mood of the bull in the foreground provides a good contrast to the placidity of the other. The bull figures have been carved in high relief in contrast with the tree which has been done in low relief. The two small dome-shaped depictions balance the composition by filling the empty space while the tree and its branches provide a nice border on the top and right. The sealing is remarkable for the skilled depiction of the bulls as well as the tree individually as also for the composition as a whole.

Acknowledgement

The author expresses his gratefulness to the authorities of State Museum, Lucknow, for providing facilities for study and supplying photograph of the seal.

NOTES

[1] H. R. Nevill, *Cawnpore, A District Gazetteer*, XIX, 1909, p. 312.

[2] No. 55, 258.

[3] *Op. cit.* [1], 312.

[4] Apparently these look like Brahmi letters *ra* a *ma* but a careful observation shows that they are hanging from the branch.

[5] *Consolidated Report on the Working of the State Museum, Lucknow*, 1960, 194.

[6] For bull in the foreground J.*J*. Marshall, *Mohenodaro and the Indus Civilization*, III, Pl. CX, no. 323; for the bull in the background, M. S , Vats, *Excavations at Harappa*, Pl. XCI, nos. 241 and 245; for tree, J. Marshall *Op. Cit.*, Pl. CXI, no. 352; Ibid, Pl. XCII, no. 3 (painted on pottery); M. S. Vats, *Op. Cit.* Pl. XCII, nos. 327 and 328; E., Mackay, *Further Excavations at Mohenjo-daro*, II, Pl. XCI, no. 4A.

[7] The tradition, however, asserts that the temple Muktadevi on the site was built in the *Treta Yuga* (Vide H. R. Nevill, *Op. Cit.*, 313). No finds of the protohistoric period have so far been reported.

[8] M. A. Suboor, ' A Note on the Babylonian Seal in Central Museum, Nagpur ', *Jr. As. Soc. Beng.*, X, no. II, N. S., 1914, 461-63, figs. 1-3.

[9] B. K. Thapar, ' Maski 1954 : A Chalcolithic Site in the Southern Deccan ', *Ancient India*, No. 13, 1957, 9, 21, 24 and n.

[10] M, Ridley, *The Seal of Aetea and the Minoan Scripts* 1963, (the pages have not been numbered).

Some Ancient Sketches In Khajuraho Temples

by DEENABANDHU PANDEY

The present note is intended to bring to notice the sketch drawings of the Khajuraho artists. Apart from the line drawings for the unfinished foliage designs depicted on the temples and plan and elevations of the temple on the floor of the *Mahāmaṇḍapa* of the Duladeva temple, there are certain interesting sketches of human and animal figures. In total, I noticed the sketches at six places. Out of these the human face of the steps of the Mātangesvara temple, the elephant on the north *Kakshāsana* of Vāmana temple and the peacock and birds on the *garbhagriha*-floor of the temple lying south of the Viśvanātha temple have been drawn in the recent past as there execution shows. Some lines of the fragmentary cela near Kandarīya temple may be of ancient days.

The most important are the sketches of the Lakshmaṇa and Devījagadambī temples. Out of the two sketches from the Lakshmaṇa temple the first one is engraved on the south plinth-wall near the eastern corner. It is an erotic picture in *paśu āsana* where the sexual intercourse between a boar and a lady is depicted [1]. Nearby it are some fishes. The boars are noted for their long-time sexual enjoyments. The second picture is also an erotic scene where a man and woman are depicted in standing pose [2]. There the lady is upside down whose legs are within the arms of the man who is trying to intercourse from the back side. The bust portion of the lady is not executed. Her left arm holds the right leg of the man and the right arm is not drawn. The face of the man is drawn in typical Khajuraho style. This picture lays on the floor of the plinth at the south west corner.

The third figure is of a person running with a lotus bud in his right hand depicted on the floor of the Mahāmaṇḍapa of the Devījagadambī temple at the north-east side-passages. The full momentum of the body is seen in the hands and legs of the man. Unfortunately the upper portion of the body is not drawn by the artist.

These sketches add something new to the known art traditions of Khajuraho.

NOTES

The author is indebted to Shri Lakshmi Kant Tripathi, Reader, Deptt. of A.I.H.C. & Arch., B.H.U. who gave him an opportunity to accompany him while his tour to Khajuraho in the Durgapuja, 1967, when he took the pencil impressions of the line drawings.

[1] It was first noticed by the author during his educational tour in 1965, organised by the Deptt. of A.I.H.C. & Arch. ,B.H.U., Cf. *Yatra ke Dina,* the tour diary submitted in part fulfilment of the Degree of Master of Arts, Deptt. of A.I.H.C. Arch., B.H.U., 1965, (unpublished).

[2] This type of *asana* is not mentioned anywhere in the literature.

ARCHAEOLOGY IN UNIVERSITIES

DECCAN COLLEGE POST-GRADUATE AND RESEARCH INSTITUTE, POONA

Since 1939 the Deccan College after it was re-started as a Post-graduate & Research Institute, has kept before it the aim of obtaining links between Pre-history and Proto-history and between Proto-history and Ancient Indian History. This was to be attempted through

(a) a study of ancient Hindu, Buddhist and Jain literature ;

(b) archaeological explorations and excavations ; and

(c) a study of the existing archaeological monuments.

In pursuance of these aims, the Deccan College began to conduct regional explorations in Maharashtra and with the encouragement given by the Government of India, it started explorations in Gujarat in 1941. Since then, the field has been enlarged to cover almost the whole of India and now during the last 28 years, parts of Maharashtra, Mysore, Andhra, U.P., M.P., Rajasthan, Karnatak and Punjab (old) have been explored by the members of the staff and post-graduate students of the Deccan College. In this work, the Institute has also obtained co-operation from the Universities of Bombay, Baroda, Karnatak and the States of Andhra, Mysore, Gujarat, M.P. and Rajasthan.

Over and above the explorations, the Institute has conducted excavations in Gujarat, Maharashtra, Mysore, Andhra, M.P. and Rajasthan. The results of these have been published. As a result of both these exploarations and excavations, the important links between Ancient history and Proto-history and between Pre-history and Proto-history, have been obtained for all these States mentioned above. In fact, we have obtained for the first time the pre-and proto-history of many of these regions.

The study of ancient monuments and the archaeology of the Deccan was completed in 1947. It was followed up by a detailed study of the Ajanta monuments entitled '*Life Depicted in the Ajanta Paintings*'. This was followed by another study, viz. '*The Study of Sanchi Monuments*'. Likewise, a study has been completed of the archaeology of three districts of U.P. and Nepal. Detailed studies have also been completed of the temples and iconography of Karnatak and Andhra.

A detailed study of the Jain literature has been completed, as also of the *Vāyu Purāṇa.* The work is proceeding on the *Agni Purāṇa.* Inscriptions have not been neglected. Historical Geography & Cultural Ethnography has been reconstructed by a study of the inscriptions of Gujarat, Maharashtra, Mysore, M.P., U.P., Rajasthan and parts of South India, viz. the Pallavas and Cholas.

After the University Grants Commission established the Department of Archaeology in the Poona University, the Institute has been able to build up an archaeological laboratory and scientific studies have been undertaken of the soils, river gravels and pottery collected from explorations and excavations. As a result of all these excavations/explorations, an up-to-date study museum has been created at the Deccan College.

—H. D. SANKALIA

UNIVERSITY OF MADRAS

The Ancient History and Archaeology department, University of Madras has taken up a scheme to find out archaeological evidence for the early history of the Lower Kaveri basin, particularly in the District of Tiruchirapalli. In pursuance of this scheme it carried out intensive explorations in the region during the last eight years from 1960 onwards, and has excavated at three sites so far :

(*a*) Tirukkampuliyur 35 miles west of Tiruchirapalli on the south bank of the river Kaveri where excavations were conducted for two seasons in 1962 and 1963.

(*b*) Alagarai, some five miles down the river on the opposite bank of the river where digging was done for one season in 1964 and

(*c*) Uraiyur, the old Chola Capital, and now within the Municipal limits of Tiruchirapalli on the south bank of the Kaveri and east bank of the stream Kodamurutti where excavations were made for three seasons during 1965, 1966 and 1967.

These continued investigations show that the first occupation of the region started in early historical times by an agricultural community making use of iron and the black-and-red and russet painted wares along with other associated wares. That rice was one of their staple food grains is proved by the occurrence of paddy husks in large quantities found in the lower levels. The occurrence of post-holes without any brick construction but associated with floor levels suggests that they lived in temporary huts probably covered with thatch. They decorated their person with beads made of terracotta, semi-precious stones, shells and rarely of paste and glass, bangles of shell etc. Their children were provided with crude clay toys.

The habitation at Tirukkampuliyur yielded, in its earliest phase, the evidence of elaborate use of painted black-and-red ware as also the russet coated painted ware which in course of time was followed by plain black-and-red ware.

The inhabitants of this period at Alagarai have left behind, besides the above traits of civilisation, a few inscribed sherds with Brahmi characters, one of which may be reconstructed to read, '*Kuttan*' meaning in Tamil, a dancer. Palaeographically the letters are very similar to those from Arikamedu and hence datable to the first or second century A. D.

The next site at Uraiyur yielded the additional evidence of a large number of inscribed sherds with Brahmi characters of the same antiquity, one of the inscriptions containing thirteen letters reading *Muppōn pēḍu Antāṇaniṉṟumāṇ* thus establishing that in the early centuries of the Christian era the Brahmi script was widely used for writing Tamil not only for engraving inscriptions in caves found in a number of places in South India but even for popular purposes like writing on potsherds in the houses of ordinary folk. Another significant fact that emerged from the diggings even at the interior site of Uraiyur is the evidence for contact with the Roman traders. Considerable numbers of rouletted ware sherds were found in the levels contemporaneous with the levels yielding the sherds with Brahmi characters and thus providing additional evidence for dating those levels to the early centuries of the Christian era. The discovery of a brick-built dyeing vat in these levels would underline the prevalence of the textile industry in which the Roman traders are known to have been engaged. Towards the end of this period occurred the evidence for the destruction of the site by floods in the river Kaveri which fact has been borne out by literature and epigraphical records of medieval times.

This first cultural period in this region came to an end with the emergence of a red slipped ware culture displacing to a great extent the earlier black-and-red ware culture. All the three sites yielded evidence of an enriched cultural equipment, in the form of mud-brick and burnt-brick residential structure with rammed structure, elaborate use of ornaments of varied types like beads made of glass, paste, shell, and semi-precious stones bangles of glass and shell, use of terracotta animal and human figurines probably some as toys, but others for cult purposes.

The large burnt-brick structure at Tirukkampuliyur, though found in ruins, revealed two rooms and a wide verandah, also exhibiting evidence of renovations more than once. The circular rubble-and-brick structure at the same site might have served as a storage bin for grain.

The occurrence of a large number of rammed floors in association with brick-and-stone debris at Uraiyur in comparable levels would indicate similar building methods at Uraiyur, in contemporary times.

All the sites, again, entered a new cultural period, the third period which was characterised by the use of an ill-fired crude red ware and marked the advent of the medieval period in South Indian history. The other cultural equipment remained more or less the same, though changes in details are noticed in many cases. But since these levels were much disturbed in all the sites not much can be said with certainty regarding the building methods, ornamentation and such other details.

—T. V. MAHALINGAM

UNIVERSITY OF SAUGAR

The Department of Ancient Indian History, Culture and Archaeology, University of Saugar, has been conducting excavations and explorations regularly since the year 1960-61. Excavations were undertaken at Eran (dist. Sagar of Madhya Pradesh) for five seasons (1960-61 to 1964-65). In the year 1965-66 the department conducted excavations at Tripuri (near Jabalpur) jointly with the Deccan College, Poona, and the M. S. University, Baroda. During the last two years the department has continued the work at Tripuri independently.

The results as obtained at the two excavated sites are briefly given here :

Eran

Eran (ancient *Airikina*), 8 miles to the south-east of Bina junction of the Central railway, stands on the southern bank of the river Bina (ancient *Veṇva*), a tributary of the Betwa. The mounds at Eran had already yielded important archaeological material in the form of coins, inscriptions, sculptures and architectural fragments. The excavations conducted during 1960-65 revealed here the existence of four main cultural periods. On the basis of the associated finds and carbon-14 dating, the chronological evidence has been found as follows :

Period I (1st quarter of the 2nd millennium B.C. to c. 700 B.C.)

Period IIA (c. 700 B. C. to c. 200 B. C.)

Period IIB (c. 200 B. C. to 1st cent. A. D.)

Period III (c. 1st century A. D. to 6th century A. D.)

Period IV (—Late Medieval upto about 1,800 A. D.)

The culture-equipment and important finds of the respective periods are described below :

Period I—This is by far the most significant period in the history of eastern Malwa, revealing the culture of the chalcolithic people. These people manufactured beautiful wheel-made painted pottery of a high type and used microliths, copper and neolithic implements. The pottery of the period includes the red ware, painted in black; coarse red ware, usually with white incised decorations; Black-and-Red ware, painted in white over the black interior; and grey ware, mostly painted in black. The finds of the period included terracotta figurines, beads, two fragments of copper celts and a thin round gold piece. The discovery of a mud defence wall and a moat is significant. The mud wall, made of black and yellow clays, enclosed the semi-circular habitation of the town from the south, the other three sides having been enclosed by the river Bina.

Period IIA—The period, beginning with the early historical time, is marked by the introduction of iron and the occurrence of Black-and-Red ware and a few sherds of N.B.P. A circular lead piece bearing the legend *raño Indagutasa* in the Asokan Brahmi characters was discovered, bringing to light the name of a new king Indragupta, who ruled in eastern Malwa in the beginning of the 2nd cent. B. C.

Period IIB—A hoard of 3,268 punch-marked coins belonging to 2nd-1st centuries B. C. was found. Two ring-wells attached to a brick floor were also discovered.

Period III—The period is marked by the emergence of red polished ware and covers the period of the Satavahanas, the western Ksatrapas and the Guptas. The coins of the period include those of the Nagas, the Ksatrapas, of Ramagupta and the Indo-Sassanian coins. Several baked clay moulds of the Ksatrapas, with the names of four kings were also unearthed. Two clay sealings also deserve notice. One of them bears the figure of *Gajalakṣmi* and the legend *Airikine Gomika visavadhikara(nasva)* written in Gupta Brahmi characters. *Airikina* stands for the old name of the town. The second sealing bears the inscription *Mahādanḍanāyaka Simhanandi.* The third sealing mentions Ksatrapa Simhasrisena, son of king Isvaramitra.

Period IV—It yielded abundance of polychrome glass and lac bangles, glazed ware sherds and coins of some native states.

Tripuri

The sequence of cultures brought to light by the excavations is as follows :

Period I—(c. 500 B.C. to 300 B.C.)
Period II—(c. 200 B.C. to 100 B.C.)
Period III—(c. 100 B.C. to 200 A. D.)
Period IV—(c. 200—400 A.D.)

Period I is marked by N. P. B., Black-and-Red, coarse red and white-slipped wares. No structural remains were noticed. A copper bull figure from the period is interesting. Period II yielded punch-marked coins, round cast coins with the Brahmi legend *Tipuri* of about 200 B. C. and inscribed Satavahana coins. These latter coins continued in Period III also. Some of them bear the legend *Raño Siri Satasa* written in bold Brahmi characters. A new king Sujethasena is known from one of the coins found in the layers of Period III. In Period IV pavements of large size burnt bricks were noticed. Several arrowheads and spear-heads made of iron and beads of glass and shell were also discovered. Among the significant finds of Period IV were six inscribed circular sealings of baked clay. Four of them mention the title *Vasisthiputra Maharaja* before the names of two rulers, Sivabodhi and Vasubodhi. These Bodhi kings ruled over the Tripuri region during the 2nd-3rd centuries A. D.

Explorations

So far the department has conducted explorations in fourteen districts of Madhya Pradesh, viz. Sagar, Vidisha, Raisen, Sehore, Mandsaur, Rewa, Satna, Panna, Jabalpur, Raigarh, Hoshangabad, Guna, Sheopuri and Gwalior. As a result, fresh material bearing on the political and religious history, and art and architecture of the region has been discovered. A detailed study of the central Indian Gupta sculpture and the Chedi and Gurjara-Pratihara art is in progress. The explorations have brought to light the fact that along with the development of the Saiva and Vaisṇava pantheons, the Śākta cult was also quite popular in major parts of Malwa and the Vindhya region during the early Medieval period.

—K. D. BAJPAI

VIKRAM UNIVERSITY, UJJAIN

Only three years ago our University opened a new branch for the Archaeological explorations and excavations so as to assist the research work in the field of indological studies. During this short time two major works were undertaken by the branch, one being the archaeological survey of ancient Ujjain and its adjacent area, the other being the small excavation of a chalcolithic site in Malwa.

The survey of Ujjain resulted in collection of images from different sites in ancient Ujjaini, ranging from the Mauryan to the Parmar period, i.e., dating back from 300 years before the Christian era to 12th and 13th century. Images of different sects of Hinduism, like Vishnu, Parwati, Uma Mahesh, Yogeshawar Vishnu, Ganesh, dancing figures, Ganga, Lakulish, Tirthankar and Yaksha are distributed throughout Ujjain. Some of them were given to the University by private collectors and enthusiasts like Padmashri Suryanarayan Vyas, Bhati, Bharati Kala Bhawan and others.

Most important of these is a figure of broken elephant which once formed the part of a Mauryan capital. The polish, which remains only at few places now, is a clear indication of its Mauryan association. This figure resembles the elephant of Sankisa. The colossalness of the figure as well as the use of Chunar stone also leads to the same conclusion. This was found at Sodhangha, an early historic site, few miles from Ujjain. This seems to be the only capital remain from Western Malwa dating to such an early peroid and associated with Asoka who ruled in Ujjain as a Governor (2nd century B.C.).

The collection was enriched by the donations of few fragmentary inscriptions. Bharati Kala Bhawan donated three inscriptions, one being of the Kshartapa period bearing the legend *Damasya raino'*. Coins of Rudradaman have often been found at Ujjain and this inscription may be that of Rudradaman. Kshatrapas ruled over Ujjain for a long time and this is the first inscription of that period ever found in Ujjain. This is a part of some railing, may be that of some stupa. The author found it in the ancient ruins of Ujjaini near Pratap Nagar. Next inscription is of the Parmar period referring to a great victory by some Parmar king Vijjasinha over some Muslim invader. It being fragmentary, no more information could be derived. The third is also a fragmentary inscription, palaeographically dating back to 8th century A.D. and referring to some battle. This was donated to Kala Bhawan by the Bhave family of Ujjain.

Following are the chalcolithic sites which were discovered while exploring Malwa within the last twenty years.

CHAMBAL VALLEY

1. Digthan.
2. Dhangawada.
3. Piplya.
4. Bhilsudi.
5. Tungani.
6. Takrawada.
7. Metwada.
8. Parmar Khedi.
9. Rajagad
10. Sanjeet.
11. Pasewa.
12. Monoti.
13. Jallod.
14. Patan.
15. Nepawali.

16. Mechakda.
17. Runija.
18. Unchakheri.
19. Thadovada.
20. Jaora.
21. Sonagad.
22. Badawada.
23. Meen.
24. Khacharoda.
25. Nạgada.
26. Rajota.
27. Dhangwada.

SHIVANA RETAM VALLEY

28. Mandsour.
29. Neemuch.
30. Baredi.

CHOTI KALISINDHA

31. Kanipura.
32. Futipul.
33. Kayatha.
34. Gangadhar.
35. Maksi.

PARWATI

36. Vidisha.
37. Betwa.

BETWA

38. Vidisha.
39. Eran.

GHAMBHIR

40. Singoda
41. Khedi.
42. Manawar.
43. Badwada.
44. Mohipura.
45. Pipalda.
46. Maheshwar.
47. Navda Toli.
48. Badada.
49. Badawada.
50. Mardana.

FEW OTHERS

51. Kithoda
52. Mahatpur.
53. Baloda.

—V. S. WAKANKAR
